# The Gospel According to
# Matthew

VERITAS

# The **Gospel** According to

# Matthew

(1:1–28:20)

Published 2010 by
Veritas Publications
7–8 Lower Abbey Street
Dublin 1
Ireland
publications@veritas.ie
www.veritas.ie

ISBN 978 1 84730 256 4

Copyright © Veritas, 2010

10 9 8 7 6 5 4 3 2

A catalogue record for this book is available from the British Library.

Designed by Norma Prause-Brewer, Veritas
Printed in Ireland by W&G Baird Ltd, Antrim

Veritas books are printed on paper made from the wood pulp of managed forests. For every tree felled, at least one tree is planted, thereby renewing natural resources.

**IMAGE USAGE**
**Mary Evans Picture Library**
pp. 8, 11, 12, 39, 40, 41, 42, 53, 58, 64, 65, 68, 69, 70, 82, 83, 84, 85, 86, 87, 88, 90, 91

# Contents

# The Gospel According to
# Matthew

## (1:1–28:20)

Guido Reni · St Matthew and the Angel · 1600s

### Introduction

The Gospel of Matthew is the first book of the New Testament and is an account of the life, ministry, death and resurrection of Jesus Christ.

The Gospel of Matthew was written between AD 70 and 85. Matthew, one of the first twelve Apostles, wrote mainly for a Jewish community, probably in Syria. He was a Jewish tax collector who left his job to join Jesus. His Gospel stresses how Jesus fulfilled Jewish prophecies and he emphasised obedience to and preservation of biblical law.

This Gospel was written in Greek at least twenty years after Mark's Gospel. Matthew's Gospel follows the outline of Mark's, with a separate section of Jesus' stories, which contains many sayings that he attributes to Jesus. Certain details of Jesus' life, of his infancy in particular, are related only in Matthew.

It was a difficult time for converts as they had to try and find a new identity as Christians and so the Gospel was written for a Church in transition. Matthew reminded them that they had hope – their hope was Jesus Christ.

The longest Gospel of the four, it is noted particularly for its rhythmical and poetic prose, making it a popular liturgical choice, and very suitable for public readings.

## THE BIRTH OF JESUS AND THE BEGINNING OF HIS MINISTRY (1:1–4:17)

**Matthew** gives a brief genealogy of Jesus of Nazareth. He also tells of his birth, his baptism by John, and the start of his ministry in Galilee.

## chapter ONE

# The Genealogy of Jesus the Messiah

An account of the genealogy of Jesus the Messiah, the son of David, the son of Abraham. ²Abraham was the father of Isaac, and Isaac the father of Jacob, and Jacob the father of Judah and his brothers, ³and Judah the father of Perez and Zerah by Tamar, and Perez the father of Hezron, and Hezron the father of Aram, ⁴and Aram the father of Aminadab, and Aminadab the father of Nahshon, and Nahshon the father of Salmon, ⁵and Salmon the father of Boaz by Rahab, and Boaz the father of Obed by Ruth, and Obed the father of Jesse, ⁶and Jesse the father of King David. And David was the father of Solomon by the wife of Uriah, ⁷and Solomon the father of Rehoboam, and Rehoboam the father of Abijah, and Abijah the father of Asaph, ⁸and Asaph the father of Jehoshaphat, and Jehoshaphat the father of Joram, and Joram the father of Uzziah, ⁹and Uzziah the father of Jotham, and Jotham the father of Ahaz, and Ahaz the father of Hezekiah, ¹⁰and Hezekiah the father of Manasseh, and Manasseh the father of Amos, and Amos the father of Josiah, ¹¹and Josiah the father of Jechoniah and his brothers, at the time of the deportation to Babylon.

¹²And after the deportation to Babylon: Jechoniah was the father of Salathiel, and Salathiel the father of Zerubbabel, ¹³and Zerubbabel the father of Abiud, and Abiud the father of Eliakim, and Eliakim the father of Azor, ¹⁴and Azor the father of Zadok, and Zadok the father of Achim, and Achim the father of Eliud, ¹⁵and Eliud the father of Eleazar, and Eleazar the father of Matthan, and Matthan the father of Jacob, ¹⁶and Jacob the father of Joseph the husband of Mary, of whom Jesus was born, who is called the Messiah. ¹⁷So all the generations from Abraham to David are fourteen generations; and from David to the deportation to Babylon, fourteen generations; and from the deportation to Babylon to the Messiah, fourteen generations.

Giovanni Bellini · Madonna · c. 1510

'She will bear a son, and you are to name him Jesus, for he will save his people from their sins.'

## The Birth of Jesus the Messiah

[18]Now the birth of Jesus the Messiah took place in this way. When his mother Mary had been engaged to Joseph, but before they lived together, she was found to be with child from the Holy Spirit. [19]Her husband Joseph, being a righteous man and unwilling to expose her to public disgrace, planned to dismiss her quietly. [20]But just when he had resolved to do this, an angel of the Lord appeared to him in a dream and said, 'Joseph, son of David, do not be afraid to take Mary as your wife, for the child conceived in her is from the Holy Spirit. [21]She will bear a son, and you are to name him Jesus, for he will save his people from their sins.' [22]All this took place to fulfil what had been spoken by the Lord through the prophet:
[23] 'Look, the virgin shall conceive and bear a son,
and they shall name him Emmanuel,'
which means, 'God is with us.' [24]When Joseph awoke from sleep, he did as the angel of the Lord commanded him; he took her as his wife, [25]but had no marital relations with her until she had borne a son; and he named him Jesus.

**Joy!**

## chapter TWO

# The Visit of the Wise Men

In the time of King Herod, after Jesus was born in Bethlehem of Judea, wise men from the East came to Jerusalem, [2]asking, 'Where is the child who has been born king of the Jews? For we observed his star at its rising, and have come to pay him homage.' [3]When King Herod heard this, he was frightened, and all Jerusalem with him; [4]and calling together all the chief priests and scribes of the people, he inquired of them where the Messiah was to be born. [5]They told him, 'In Bethlehem of Judea; for so it has been written by the prophet:
[6]"And you, Bethlehem, in the land of Judah, are by no means least among the rulers of Judah;
for from you shall come a ruler who is to shepherd my people Israel."'
[7]Then Herod secretly called for the wise men and learned from them the exact time when the star had appeared. [8]Then he sent them to Bethlehem, saying, 'Go and search diligently for the child; and when you have found him, bring me word so that I may also go and pay him homage.'
[9]When they had heard the king, they set out; and there, ahead of them, went the star that they had seen at its rising, until it stopped over the place where the child was. [10]When they saw that the star had stopped, they were overwhelmed with joy.

# Out of Egypt!

Albrecht Dürer · The Seven Sorrows of the Virgin: The Flight into Egypt · c. 1496

¹¹On entering the house, they saw the child with Mary his mother; and they knelt down and paid him homage. Then, opening their treasure chests, they offered him gifts of gold, frankincense, and myrrh. ¹²And having been warned in a dream not to return to Herod, they left for their own country by another road.

## The Escape to Egypt

¹³Now after they had left, an angel of the Lord appeared to Joseph in a dream and said, 'Get up, take the child and his mother, and flee to Egypt, and remain there until I tell you; for Herod is about to search for the child, to destroy him.' ¹⁴Then Joseph got up, took the child and his mother by night, and went to Egypt, ¹⁵and remained there until the death of Herod. This was to fulfil what had been spoken by the Lord through the prophet, 'Out of Egypt I have called my son.'

## The Massacre of the Infants

¹⁶When Herod saw that he had been tricked by the wise men, he was infuriated, and he sent and killed all the children in and around Bethlehem who were two years old or under, according to the time that he had learned from the wise men. ¹⁷Then was fulfilled what had been spoken through the prophet Jeremiah:
¹⁸'A voice was heard in Ramah,
wailing and loud lamentation,
Rachel weeping for her children;
she refused to be consoled, because they are no more.'

## The Return from Egypt

¹⁹When Herod died, an angel of the Lord suddenly appeared in a dream to Joseph in Egypt and said, ²⁰'Get up, take the child and his mother, and go to the land of Israel, for those who were seeking the child's life are dead.' ²¹Then Joseph got up, took the child and his mother, and went to the land of Israel. ²²But when he heard that Archelaus was ruling over Judea in place of his father Herod, he was afraid to go there. And after being warned in a dream, he went away to the district of Galilee. ²³There he made his home in a town called Nazareth, so that what had been spoken through the prophets might be fulfilled, 'He will be called a Nazorean.'

'He will be called a Nazorean.'

Bartolomé Esteban Perez Murillo · The Holy Children with a Shell · c. 17th Century

## chapter THREE

'Prepare the way of the Lord ...'

# The Proclamation of John the Baptist

In those days John the Baptist appeared in the wilderness of Judea, proclaiming, [2]'Repent, for the kingdom of heaven has come near.' [3]This is the one of whom the prophet Isaiah spoke when he said,
'The voice of one crying out in the wilderness:
"Prepare the way of the Lord,
make his paths straight."'

[4]Now John wore clothing of camel's hair with a leather belt around his waist, and his food was locusts and wild honey. [5]Then the people of Jerusalem and all Judea were going out to him, and all the region along the Jordan, [6]and they were baptised by him in the river Jordan, confessing their sins.

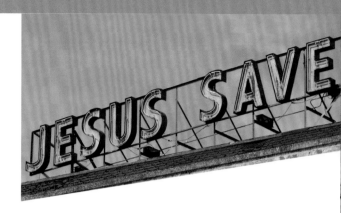

7But when he saw many Pharisees and Sadducees coming for baptism, he said to them, 'You brood of vipers! Who warned you to flee from the wrath to come? 8Bear fruit worthy of repentance. 9Do not presume to say to yourselves, "We have Abraham as our ancestor"; for I tell you, God is able from these stones to raise up children to Abraham. 10Even now the axe is lying at the root of the trees; every tree therefore that does not bear good fruit is cut down and thrown into the fire. 11"I baptise you with water for repentance, but one who is more powerful than I is coming after me; I am not worthy to carry his sandals. He will baptise you with the Holy Spirit and fire. 12His winnowing fork is in his hand, and he will clear his threshing floor and will gather his wheat into the granary; but the chaff he will burn with unquenchable fire.'

## The Baptism of Jesus

13Then Jesus came from Galilee to John at the Jordan, to be baptised by him. 14John would have prevented him, saying, 'I need to be baptised by you, and do you come to me?' 15But Jesus answered him, 'Let it be so now; for it is proper for us in this way to fulfil all righteousness.' Then he consented. 16And when Jesus had been baptised, just as he came up from the water, suddenly the heavens were opened to him and he saw the Spirit of God descending like a dove and alighting on him. 17And a voice from heaven said, 'This is my Son, the Beloved, with whom I am well pleased.'

## chapter FOUR

# The **Temptation** of Jesus

Then Jesus was led up by the Spirit into the wilderness to be tempted by the devil. ²He fasted forty days and forty nights, and afterwards he was famished. ³The tempter came and said to him, 'If you are the Son of God, command these stones to become loaves of bread.' ⁴But he answered, 'It is written,
"One does not live by bread alone,
but by every word that comes from the mouth of God."'
⁵Then the devil took him to the holy city and placed him on the pinnacle of the temple, ⁶saying to him, 'If you are the Son of God, throw yourself down; for it is written,
"He will command his angels concerning you,"
and "On their hands they will bear you up,
so that you will not dash your foot against a stone."' ⁷Jesus said to him, 'Again it is written,
"Do not put the Lord your God to the test."'
⁸Again, the devil took him to a very high mountain and showed him all the kingdoms of the world and their splendour; ⁹and he said to him, 'All these I will give you, if you will fall down and worship me.' ¹⁰Jesus said to him, 'Away with you, Satan! for it is written,
"Worship the Lord your God,
and serve only him."' ¹¹Then the devil left him, and suddenly angels came and waited on him.

> 'Worship the Lord your God, and serve only him.'

# Jesus Begins His **Ministry in Galilee**

¹²Now when Jesus heard that John had been arrested, he withdrew to Galilee. ¹³He left Nazareth and made his home in Capernaum by the sea, in the territory of Zebulun and Naphtali, ¹⁴so that what had been spoken through the prophet Isaiah might be fulfilled:
¹⁵'Land of Zebulun, land of Naphtali,
on the road by the sea, across the Jordan,
Galilee of the Gentiles –
¹⁶the people who sat in darkness have seen a great light,
and for those who sat in the region and shadow of death
light has dawned.' ¹⁷From that time Jesus began to proclaim,
'Repent, for the kingdom of heaven has come near.'

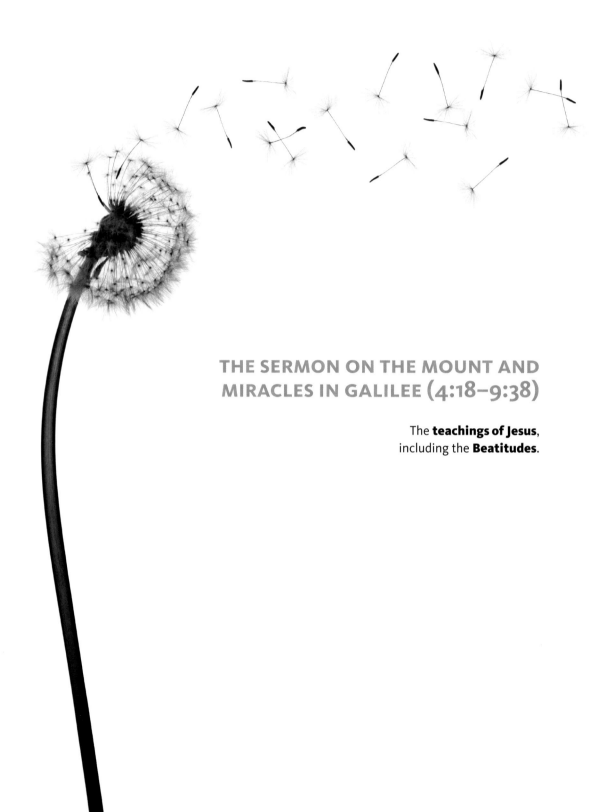

# THE SERMON ON THE MOUNT AND MIRACLES IN GALILEE (4:18–9:38)

The **teachings of Jesus**, including the **Beatitudes**.

## Jesus Calls the First Disciples

[18]As he walked by the Sea of Galilee, he saw two brothers, Simon, who is called Peter, and Andrew his brother, casting a net into the sea – for they were fishermen. [19]And he said to them, 'Follow me, and I will make you fish for people.' [20]Immediately they left their nets and followed him. [21]As he went from there, he saw two other brothers, James son of Zebedee and his brother John, in the boat with their father Zebedee, mending their nets, and he called them. [22]Immediately they left the boat and their father, and followed him.

## Jesus Ministers to Crowds of People

[23]Jesus went throughout Galilee, teaching in their synagogues and proclaiming the good news of the kingdom and curing every disease and every sickness among the people. [24]So his fame spread throughout all Syria, and they brought to him all the sick, those who were afflicted with various diseases and pains, demoniacs, epileptics, and paralytics, and he cured them. [25]And great crowds followed him from Galilee, the Decapolis, Jerusalem, Judea, and from beyond the Jordan.

'Follow me, and I will make you fish for people.'

## chapter FIVE

# The
# Beatitudes

When Jesus saw the crowds, he went up the mountain; and after he sat down, his disciples came to him. ²Then he began to speak, and taught them, saying:

³'Blessed are the poor in spirit, for theirs is the kingdom of heaven.

⁴'Blessed are those who mourn, for they will be comforted.

⁵'Blessed are the meek, for they will inherit the earth.

⁶'Blessed are those who hunger and thirst for righteousness, for they will be filled.

⁷'Blessed are the merciful, for they will receive mercy.

⁸'Blessed are the pure in heart, for they will see God.

⁹'Blessed are the peacemakers, for they will be called children of God.

¹⁰'Blessed are those who are persecuted for righteousness' sake, for theirs is the kingdom of heaven.

¹¹'Blessed are you when people revile you and persecute you and utter all kinds of evil against you falsely on my account. ¹²Rejoice and be glad, for your reward is great in heaven, for in the same way they persecuted the prophets who were before you.

## Salt and Light

¹³'You are the salt of the earth; but if salt has lost its taste, how can its saltiness be restored? It is no longer good for anything, but is thrown out and trampled under foot.

¹⁴'You are the light of the world. A city built on a hill cannot be hid. ¹⁵No one after lighting a lamp puts it under the bushel basket, but on the lampstand, and it gives light to all in the house. ¹⁶In the same way, let your light shine before others, so that they may see your good works and give glory to your Father in heaven.

# Blessed!
# are you!

# Concerning Anger

²¹"You have heard that it was said to those of ancient times, "You shall not murder"; and "whoever murders shall be liable to judgement." ²²But I say to you that if you are angry with a brother or sister, you will be liable to judgement; and if you insult a brother or sister, you will be liable to the council; and if you say, "You fool", you will be liable to the hell of fire. ²³So when you are offering your gift at the altar, if you remember that your brother or sister has something against you, ²⁴leave your gift there before the altar and go; first be reconciled to your brother or sister, and then come and offer your gift. ²⁵Come to terms quickly with your accuser while you are on the way to court with him, or your accuser may hand you over to the judge, and the judge to the guard, and you will be thrown into prison. ²⁶Truly I tell you, you will never get out until you have paid the last penny.

# The Law and the Prophets

¹⁷'Do not think that I have come to abolish the law or the prophets; I have come not to abolish but to fulfil. ¹⁸For truly I tell you, until heaven and earth pass away, not one letter, not one stroke of a letter, will pass from the law until all is accomplished. ¹⁹Therefore, whoever breaks one of the least of these commandments, and teaches others to do the same, will be called least in the kingdom of heaven; but whoever does them and teaches them will be called great in the kingdom of heaven. ²⁰For I tell you, unless your righteousness exceeds that of the scribes and Pharisees, you will never enter the kingdom of heaven.

# Concerning Adultery

²⁷'You have heard that it was said, "You shall not commit adultery." ²⁸But I say to you that everyone who looks at a woman with lust has already committed adultery with her in his heart. ²⁹If your right eye causes you to sin, tear it out and throw it away; it is better for you to lose one of your members than for your whole body to be thrown into hell. ³⁰And if your right hand causes you to sin, cut it off and throw it away; it is better for you to lose one of your members than for your whole body to go into hell.

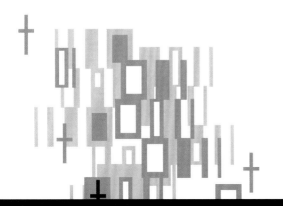

## Concerning Divorce

[31]"It was also said, "Whoever divorces his wife, let him give her a certificate of divorce." [32]But I say to you that anyone who divorces his wife, except on the ground of unchastity, causes her to commit adultery; and whoever marries a divorced woman commits adultery.

## Concerning Oaths

[33]'Again, you have heard that it was said to those of ancient times, "You shall not swear falsely, but carry out the vows you have made to the Lord." [34]But I say to you, Do not swear at all, either by heaven, for it is the throne of God, [35]or by the earth, for it is his footstool, or by Jerusalem, for it is the city of the great King. [36]And do not swear by your head, for you cannot make one hair white or black. [37]Let your word be "Yes, Yes" or "No, No"; anything more than this comes from the evil one.

## Concerning Retaliation

[38]'You have heard that it was said, "An eye for an eye and a tooth for a tooth." [39]But I say to you, Do not resist an evildoer. But if anyone strikes you on the right cheek, turn the other also; [40]and if anyone wants to sue you and take your coat, give your cloak as well; [41]and if anyone forces you to go one mile, go also the second mile. [42]Give to everyone who begs from you, and do not refuse anyone who wants to borrow from you.

## Love for Enemies

43"You have heard that it was said, "You shall love your neighbour and hate your enemy." 44But I say to you, Love your enemies and pray for those who persecute you, 45so that you may be children of your Father in heaven; for he makes his sun rise on the evil and on the good, and sends rain on the righteous and on the unrighteous. 46For if you love those who love you, what reward do you have? Do not even the tax collectors do the same? 47And if you greet only your brothers and sisters, what more are you doing than others? Do not even the Gentiles do the same? 48Be perfect, therefore, as your heavenly Father is perfect.

## chapter SIX

## Concerning Almsgiving

'Beware of practising your piety before others in order to be seen by them; for then you have no reward from your Father in heaven. 2'So whenever you give alms, do not sound a trumpet before you, as the hypocrites do in the synagogues and in the streets, so that they may be praised by others. Truly I tell you, they have received their reward. 3But when you give alms, do not let your left hand know what your right hand is doing, 4so that your alms may be done in secret; and your Father who sees in secret will reward you.

## Concerning Prayer

5'And whenever you pray, do not be like the hypocrites; for they love to stand and pray in the synagogues and at the street corners, so that they may be seen by others. Truly I tell you, they have received their reward. 6But whenever you pray, go into your room and shut the door and pray to your Father who is in secret; and your Father who sees in secret will reward you. 7'When you are praying, do not heap up empty phrases as the Gentiles do; for they think that they will be heard because of their many words. 8Do not be like them, for your Father knows what you need before you ask him.
9'Pray then in this way:
Our Father in heaven,
hallowed be your name.
10Your kingdom come.
Your will be done, on earth as it is in heaven.
11Give us this day our daily bread.
12And forgive us our debts,
as we also have forgiven our debtors.
13And do not bring us to the time of trial,
but rescue us from the evil one. 14For if you forgive others their trespasses, your heavenly Father will also forgive you; 15but if you do not forgive others, neither will your Father forgive your trespasses.

Forgive Love

'... do not let your left hand know what your right hand is doing ...'

## Concerning Fasting

[16]'And whenever you fast, do not look dismal, like the hypocrites, for they disfigure their faces so as to show others that they are fasting. Truly I tell you, they have received their reward. [17]But when you fast, put oil on your head and wash your face, [18]so that your fasting may be seen not by others but by your Father who is in secret; and your Father who sees in secret will reward you.

## Concerning Treasures

[19]'Do not store up for yourselves treasures on earth, where moth and rust consume and where thieves break in and steal; [20]but store up for yourselves treasures in heaven, where neither moth nor rust consumes and where thieves do not break in and steal. [21]For where your treasure is, there your heart will be also.

## The Sound Eye

[22]'The eye is the lamp of the body. So, if your eye is healthy, your whole body will be full of light; [23]but if your eye is unhealthy, your whole body will be full of darkness. If then the light in you is darkness, how great is the darkness!

## Serving Two Masters

[24]'No one can serve two masters; for a slave will either hate the one and love the other, or be devoted to the one and despise the other. You cannot serve God and wealth.

## Do Not Worry

[25]'Therefore I tell you, do not worry about your life, what you will eat or what you will drink, or about your body, what you will wear. Is not life more than food, and the body more than clothing? [26]Look at the birds of the air; they neither sow nor reap nor gather into barns, and yet your heavenly Father feeds them. Are you not of more value than they? [27]And can any of you by worrying add a single hour to your span of life? [28]And why do you worry about clothing? Consider the lilies of the field, how they grow; they neither toil nor spin, [29]yet I tell you, even Solomon in all his glory was not clothed like one of these. [30]But if God so clothes the grass of the field, which is alive today and tomorrow is thrown into the oven, will he not much more clothe you – you of little faith? [31]Therefore do not worry, saying, "What will we eat?" or "What will we drink?" or "What will we wear?" [32]For it is the Gentiles who strive for all these things; and indeed your heavenly Father knows that you need all these things. [33]But strive first for the kingdom of God and his righteousness, and all these things will be given to you as well. [34]'So do not worry about tomorrow, for tomorrow will bring worries of its own. Today's trouble is enough for today.

'In everything do to others as you would have them do to you; for this is the law and the prophets.'

## chapter SEVEN

# Judging Others

'Do not judge, so that you may not be judged. ²For with the judgement you make you will be judged, and the measure you give will be the measure you get. ³Why do you see the speck in your neighbour's eye, but do not notice the log in your own eye? ⁴Or how can you say to your neighbour, "Let me take the speck out of your eye", while the log is in your own eye? ⁵You hypocrite, first take the log out of your own eye, and then you will see clearly to take the speck out of your neighbour's eye.

# Profaning the Holy

⁶'Do not give what is holy to dogs; and do not throw your pearls before swine, or they will trample them under foot and turn and maul you.

# Ask, Search, Knock

⁷'Ask, and it will be given you; search, and you will find; knock, and the door will be opened for you. ⁸For everyone who asks receives, and everyone who searches finds, and for everyone who knocks, the door will be opened. ⁹Is there anyone among you who, if your child asks for bread, will give a stone? ¹⁰Or if the child asks for a fish, will give a snake? ¹¹If you then, who are evil, know how to give good gifts to your children, how much more will your Father in heaven give good things to those who ask him!

# The Golden Rule

¹²'In everything do to others as you would have them do to you; for this is the law and the prophets.

# The Narrow Gate

¹³'Enter through the narrow gate; for the gate is wide and the road is easy that leads to destruction, and there are many who take it. ¹⁴For the gate is narrow and the road is hard that leads to life, and there are few who find it.

Ask

Receive

## Concerning **Self-Deception**

²¹"Not everyone who says to me, "Lord, Lord", will enter the kingdom of heaven, but only the one who does the will of my Father in heaven. ²²On that day many will say to me, "Lord, Lord, did we not prophesy in your name, and cast out demons in your name, and do many deeds of power in your name?" ²³Then I will declare to them, "I never knew you; go away from me, you evildoers."

## A **Tree** and Its **Fruit**

¹⁵"Beware of false prophets, who come to you in sheep's clothing but inwardly are ravenous wolves. ¹⁶You will know them by their fruits. Are grapes gathered from thorns, or figs from thistles? ¹⁷In the same way, every good tree bears good fruit, but the bad tree bears bad fruit. ¹⁸A good tree cannot bear bad fruit, nor can a bad tree bear good fruit. ¹⁹Every tree that does not bear good fruit is cut down and thrown into the fire. ²⁰Thus you will know them by their fruits.

# Hearers and Doers

24'Everyone then who hears these words of mine and acts on them will be like a wise man who built his house on rock. 25The rain fell, the floods came, and the winds blew and beat on that house, but it did not fall, because it had been founded on rock. 26And everyone who hears these words of mine and does not act on them will be like a foolish man who built his house on sand. 27The rain fell, and the floods came, and the winds blew and beat against that house, and it fell – and great was its fall!'
28Now when Jesus had finished saying these things, the crowds were astounded at his teaching, 29for he taught them as one having authority, and not as their scribes.

'Everyone then who hears these words of mine and acts on them will be like a wise man who built his house on rock.'

Duccio di Buoninsegna · The Healing of the Blind Man · 1308–1311

## chapter EIGHT

# Jesus Cleanses a Leper

When Jesus had come down from the mountain, great crowds followed him; ²and there was a leper who came to him and knelt before him, saying, 'Lord, if you choose, you can make me clean.' ³He stretched out his hand and touched him, saying, 'I do choose. Be made clean!' Immediately his leprosy was cleansed. ⁴Then Jesus said to him, 'See that you say nothing to anyone; but go, show yourself to the priest, and offer the gift that Moses commanded, as a testimony to them.'

Paris Psalter · Byzantine Illuminated Manuscript · c. 10th century

## Jesus Heals Many at Peter's House

¹⁴When Jesus entered Peter's house, he saw his mother-in-law lying in bed with a fever; ¹⁵he touched her hand, and the fever left her, and she got up and began to serve him. ¹⁶That evening they brought to him many who were possessed with demons; and he cast out the spirits with a word, and cured all who were sick. ¹⁷This was to fulfil what had been spoken through the prophet Isaiah, 'He took our infirmities and bore our diseases.'

## Jesus Heals a Centurion's Servant

⁵When he entered Capernaum, a centurion came to him, appealing to him ⁶and saying, 'Lord, my servant is lying at home paralysed, in terrible distress.' ⁷And he said to him, 'I will come and cure him.' ⁸The centurion answered, 'Lord, I am not worthy to have you come under my roof; but only speak the word, and my servant will be healed. ⁹For I also am a man under authority, with soldiers under me; and I say to one, "Go", and he goes, and to another, "Come", and he comes, and to my slave, "Do this", and the slave does it.' ¹⁰When Jesus heard him, he was amazed and said to those who followed him, 'Truly I tell you, in no one in Israel have I found such faith. ¹¹I tell you, many will come from east and west and will eat with Abraham and Isaac and Jacob in the kingdom of heaven, ¹²while the heirs of the kingdom will be thrown into the outer darkness, where there will be weeping and gnashing of teeth.' ¹³And to the centurion Jesus said, 'Go; let it be done for you according to your faith.' And the servant was healed in that hour.

## Would-Be Followers of Jesus

¹⁸Now when Jesus saw great crowds around him, he gave orders to go over to the other side. ¹⁹A scribe then approached and said, 'Teacher, I will follow you wherever you go.' ²⁰And Jesus said to him, 'Foxes have holes, and birds of the air have nests; but the Son of Man has nowhere to lay his head.' ²¹Another of his disciples said to him, 'Lord, first let me go and bury my father.' ²²But Jesus said to him, 'Follow me, and let the dead bury their own dead.'

## Jesus Stills the Storm

<sup>23</sup>And when he got into the boat, his disciples followed him. <sup>24</sup>A windstorm arose on the sea, so great that the boat was being swamped by the waves; but he was asleep. <sup>25</sup>And they went and woke him up, saying, 'Lord, save us! We are perishing!' <sup>26</sup>And he said to them, 'Why are you afraid, you of little faith?' Then he got up and rebuked the winds and the sea; and there was a dead calm. <sup>27</sup>They were amazed, saying, 'What sort of man is this, that even the winds and the sea obey him?'

## Jesus Heals the Gadarene Demoniacs

<sup>28</sup>When he came to the other side, to the country of the Gadarenes, two demoniacs coming out of the tombs met him. They were so fierce that no one could pass that way. <sup>29</sup>Suddenly they shouted, 'What have you to do with us, Son of God? Have you come here to torment us before the time?' <sup>30</sup>Now a large herd of swine was feeding at some distance from them. <sup>31</sup>The demons begged him, 'If you cast us out, send us into the herd of swine.' <sup>32</sup>And he said to them, 'Go!' So they came out and entered the swine; and suddenly, the whole herd rushed down the steep bank into the sea and perished in the water. <sup>33</sup>The swineherds ran off, and on going into the town, they told the whole story about what had happened to the demoniacs. <sup>34</sup>Then the whole town came out to meet Jesus; and when they saw him, they begged him to leave their neighbourhood.

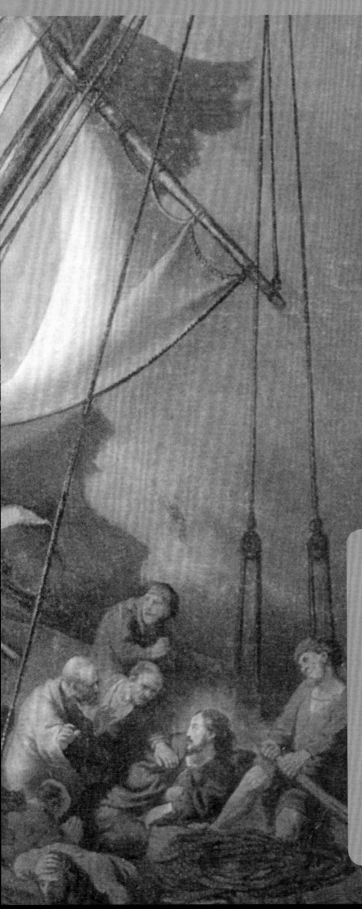

## chapter NINE

### Jesus Heals a Paralytic

And after getting into a boat he crossed the sea and came to his own town. ²And just then some people were carrying a paralysed man lying on a bed. When Jesus saw their faith, he said to the paralytic, 'Take heart, son; your sins are forgiven.' ³Then some of the scribes said to themselves, 'This man is blaspheming.' ⁴But Jesus, perceiving their thoughts, said, 'Why do you think evil in your hearts? ⁵For which is easier, to say, "Your sins are forgiven", or to say, "Stand up and walk"? ⁶But so that you may know that the Son of Man has authority on earth to forgive sins' – he then said to the paralytic – 'stand up, take your bed and go to your home.' ⁷And he stood up and went to his home. ⁸When the crowds saw it, they were filled with awe, and they glorified God, who had given such authority to human beings.

### The Call of Matthew

⁹As Jesus was walking along, he saw a man called Matthew sitting at the tax booth; and he said to him, 'Follow me.' And he got up and followed him.
¹⁰And as he sat at dinner in the house, many tax collectors and sinners came and were sitting with him and his disciples. ¹¹When the Pharisees saw this, they said to his disciples, 'Why does your teacher eat with tax collectors and sinners?' ¹²But when he heard this, he said, 'Those who are well have no need of a physician, but those who are sick. ¹³Go and learn what this means, "I desire mercy, not sacrifice." For I have come to call not the righteous but sinners.'

Rembrandt van Rijn · The Storm on the Sea of Galilee · 1633

## The Question about **Fasting**

[14]Then the disciples of John came to him, saying, 'Why do we and the Pharisees fast often, but your disciples do not fast?' [15]And Jesus said to them, 'The wedding guests cannot mourn as long as the bridegroom is with them, can they? The days will come when the bridegroom is taken away from them, and then they will fast. [16]No one sews a piece of unshrunk cloth on an old cloak, for the patch pulls away from the cloak, and a worse tear is made. [17]Neither is new wine put into old wineskins; otherwise, the skins burst, and the wine is spilled, and the skins are destroyed; but new wine is put into fresh wineskins, and so both are preserved.'

## **A Girl Restored** to Life and a Woman Healed

[18]While he was saying these things to them, suddenly a leader of the synagogue came in and knelt before him, saying, 'My daughter has just died; but come and lay your hand on her, and she will live.' [19]And Jesus got up and followed him, with his disciples. [20]Then suddenly a woman who had been suffering from haemorrhages for twelve years came up behind him and touched the fringe of his cloak, [21]for she said to herself, 'If I only touch his cloak, I will be made well.' [22]Jesus turned, and seeing her he said, 'Take heart, daughter; your faith has made you well.' And instantly the woman was made well. [23]When Jesus came to the leader's house and saw the flute players and the crowd making a commotion, [24]he said, 'Go

away; for the girl is not dead but sleeping.' And they laughed at him. [25]But when the crowd had been put outside, he went in and took her by the hand, and the girl got up. [26]And the report of this spread throughout that district.

## **Jesus Heals** Two Blind Men

[27]As Jesus went on from there, two blind men followed him, crying loudly, 'Have mercy on us, Son of David!' [28]When he entered the house, the blind men came to him; and Jesus said to them, 'Do you believe that I am able to do this?' They said to him, 'Yes, Lord.' [29]Then he touched their eyes and said, 'According to your faith let it be done to you.' [30]And their eyes were opened. Then Jesus sternly ordered them, 'See that no one knows of this.' [31]But they went away and spread the news about him throughout that district.

## **Jesus Heals**
'Never has anything like this been seen in Israel.'

# Rejoice!

## Jesus Heals One Who Was Mute

³²After they had gone away, a demoniac who was mute was brought to him. ³³And when the demon had been cast out, the one who had been mute spoke; and the crowds were amazed and said, 'Never has anything like this been seen in Israel.' ³⁴But the Pharisees said, 'By the ruler of the demons he casts out the demons.'

## The Harvest is Great, the Labourers Few

³⁵Then Jesus went about all the cities and villages, teaching in their synagogues, and proclaiming the good news of the kingdom, and curing every disease and every sickness. ³⁶When he saw the crowds, he had compassion for them, because they were harassed and helpless, like sheep without a shepherd. ³⁷Then he said to his disciples, 'The harvest is plentiful, but the labourers are few; ³⁸therefore ask the Lord of the harvest to send out labourers into his harvest.'

# THE APOSTLES AND THE TEACHINGS OF JESUS (10:1–12:50)

**Jesus gathers his Twelve** and continues his teachings.

## chapter TEN

# The Twelve Apostles

Then Jesus summoned his twelve disciples and gave them authority over unclean spirits, to cast them out, and to cure every disease and every sickness. [2]These are the names of the twelve apostles: first, Simon, also known as Peter, and his brother Andrew; James son of Zebedee, and his brother John; [3]Philip and Bartholomew; Thomas and Matthew the tax collector; James son of Alphaeus, and Thaddaeus; [4]Simon the Cananaean, and Judas Iscariot, the one who betrayed him.

# The Mission of the Twelve

[5]These twelve Jesus sent out with the following instructions: 'Go nowhere among the Gentiles, and enter no town of the Samaritans, [6]but go rather to the lost sheep of the house of Israel. [7]As you go, proclaim the good news, "The kingdom of heaven has come near." [8]Cure the sick, raise the dead, cleanse the lepers, cast out demons. You received without payment; give without payment. [9]Take no gold, or silver, or copper in your belts, [10]no bag for your journey, or two tunics, or sandals, or a staff; for labourers deserve their food. [11]Whatever town or village you enter, find out who in it is worthy, and stay there until you leave. [12]As you enter the house, greet it. [13]If the house is worthy, let your peace come upon it; but if it is not worthy, let your peace return to you. [14]If anyone will not welcome you or listen to your words, shake off the dust from your feet as you leave that house or town. [15]Truly I tell you, it will be more tolerable for the land of Sodom and Gomorrah on the day of judgement than for that town.

## Coming Persecutions

[16]'See, I am sending you out like sheep into the midst of wolves; so be wise as serpents and innocent as doves. [17]Beware of them, for they will hand you over to councils and flog you in their synagogues; [18]and you will be dragged before governors and kings because of me, as a testimony to them and the Gentiles. [19]When they hand you over, do not worry about how you are to speak or what you are to say; for what you are to say will be given to you at that time; [20]for it is not you who speak, but the Spirit of your Father speaking through you. [21]Brother will betray brother to death, and a father his child, and children will rise against parents and have them put to death; [22]and you will be hated by all because of my name. But the one who endures to the end will be saved. [23]When they persecute you in one town, flee to the next; for truly I tell you, you will not have gone through all the towns of Israel before the Son of Man comes.

[24]'A disciple is not above the teacher, nor a slave above the master; [25]it is enough for the disciple to be like the teacher, and the slave like the master. If they have called the master of the house Beelzebul, how much more will they malign those of his household!

## Whom to **Fear**

²⁶'So have no fear of them; for nothing is covered up that will not be uncovered, and nothing secret that will not become known. ²⁷What I say to you in the dark, tell in the light; and what you hear whispered, proclaim from the housetops. ²⁸Do not fear those who kill the body but cannot kill the soul; rather fear him who can destroy both soul and body in hell. ²⁹Are not two sparrows sold for a penny? Yet not one of them will fall to the ground apart from your Father. ³⁰And even the hairs of your head are all counted. ³¹So do not be afraid; you are of more value than many sparrows. ³²'Everyone therefore who acknowledges me before others, I also will acknowledge before my Father in heaven; ³³but whoever denies me before others, I also will deny before my Father in heaven.

## **Not Peace**, but a Sword

³⁴'Do not think that I have come to bring peace to the earth; I have not come to bring peace, but a sword. ³⁵For I have come to set a man against his father, and a daughter against her mother, and a daughter-in-law against her mother-in-law; ³⁶and one's foes will be members of one's own household. ³⁷Whoever loves father or mother more than me is not worthy of me; and whoever loves son or daughter more than me is not worthy of me; ³⁸and whoever does not take up the cross and follow me is not worthy of me. ³⁹Those who find their life will lose it, and those who lose their life for my sake will find it.

## Rewards

⁴⁰'Whoever welcomes you welcomes me, and whoever welcomes me welcomes the one who sent me. ⁴¹Whoever welcomes a prophet in the name of a prophet will receive a prophet's reward; and whoever welcomes a righteous person in the name of a righteous person will receive the reward of the righteous; ⁴²and whoever gives even a cup of cold water to one of these little ones in the name of a disciple – truly I tell you, none of these will lose their reward.'

# Proclaim from the housetops!

## Jesus Praises John the Baptist

⁷As they went away, Jesus began to speak to the crowds about John: 'What did you go out into the wilderness to look at? A reed shaken by the wind? ⁸What then did you go out to see? Someone dressed in soft robes? Look, those who wear soft robes are in royal palaces. ⁹What then did you go out to see? A prophet? Yes, I tell you, and more than a prophet. ¹⁰This is the one about whom it is written,
"See, I am sending my messenger ahead of you, who will prepare your way before you."
¹¹Truly I tell you, among those born of women no one has arisen greater than John the Baptist; yet the least in the kingdom of heaven is greater than he. ¹²From the days of John the Baptist until now the kingdom of heaven has suffered violence, and the violent take it by force. ¹³For all the prophets and the law prophesied until John came; ¹⁴and if you are willing to accept it, he is Elijah who is to come. ¹⁵Let anyone with ears listen!
¹⁶'But to what will I compare this generation? It is like children sitting in the marketplaces and calling to one another,
¹⁷"We played the flute for you, and you did not dance;
we wailed, and you did not mourn."
¹⁸For John came neither eating nor drinking, and they say, "He has a demon"; ¹⁹the Son of Man came eating and drinking, and they say, "Look, a glutton and a drunkard, a friend of tax collectors and sinners!" Yet wisdom is vindicated by her deeds.'

## chapter ELEVEN

Now when Jesus had finished instructing his twelve disciples, he went on from there to teach and proclaim his message in their cities.

## Messengers from John the Baptist

²When John heard in prison what the Messiah was doing, he sent word by his disciples ³and said to him, 'Are you the one who is to come, or are we to wait for another?' ⁴Jesus answered them, 'Go and tell John what you hear and see: ⁵the blind receive their sight, the lame walk, the lepers are cleansed, the deaf hear, the dead are raised, and the poor have good news brought to them. ⁶And blessed is anyone who takes no offence at me.'

'Let anyone with ears listen!'

## Woes to Unrepentant Cities

<sup>20</sup>Then he began to reproach the cities in which most of his deeds of power had been done, because they did not repent. <sup>21</sup>"Woe to you, Chorazin! Woe to you, Bethsaida! For if the deeds of power done in you had been done in Tyre and Sidon, they would have repented long ago in sackcloth and ashes. <sup>22</sup>But I tell you, on the day of judgement it will be more tolerable for Tyre and Sidon than for you. <sup>23</sup>And you, Capernaum,
will you be exalted to heaven?
No, you will be brought down to Hades. For if the deeds of power done in you had been done in Sodom, it would have remained until this day. <sup>24</sup>But I tell you that on the day of judgement it will be more tolerable for the land of Sodom than for you.'

## Jesus Thanks His Father

<sup>25</sup>At that time Jesus said, 'I thank you, Father, Lord of heaven and earth, because you have hidden these things from the wise and the intelligent and have revealed them to infants; <sup>26</sup>yes, Father, for such was your gracious will. <sup>27</sup>All things have been handed over to me by my Father; and no one knows the Son except the Father, and no one knows the Father except the Son and anyone to whom the Son chooses to reveal him. <sup>28</sup>'Come to me, all you that are weary and are carrying heavy burdens, and I will give you rest. <sup>29</sup>Take my yoke upon you, and learn from me; for I am gentle and humble in heart, and you will find rest for your souls. <sup>30</sup>For my yoke is easy, and my burden is light.'

## chapter TWELVE

## Plucking Grain on the Sabbath

At that time Jesus went through the grainfields on the sabbath; his disciples were hungry, and they began to pluck heads of grain and to eat. <sup>2</sup>When the Pharisees saw it, they said to him, 'Look, your disciples are doing what is not lawful to do on the sabbath.' <sup>3</sup>He said to them, 'Have you not read what David did when he and his companions were hungry? <sup>4</sup>He entered the house of God and ate the bread of the Presence, which it was not lawful for him or his companions to eat, but only for the priests. <sup>5</sup>Or have you not read in the law that on the sabbath the priests in the temple break the sabbath and yet are guiltless? <sup>6</sup>I tell you, something greater than the temple is here. <sup>7</sup>But if you had known what this means, "I desire mercy and not sacrifice," you would not have condemned the guiltless. <sup>8</sup>For the Son of Man is lord of the sabbath.'

## The Man with a Withered Hand

<sup>9</sup>He left that place and entered their synagogue; <sup>10</sup>a man was there with a withered hand, and they asked him, 'Is it lawful to cure on the sabbath?' so that they might accuse him. <sup>11</sup>He said to them, 'Suppose one of you has only one sheep and it falls into a pit on the sabbath; will you not lay hold of it and lift it out? <sup>12</sup>How much more valuable is a human being than a sheep! So it is lawful to do good on the sabbath.' <sup>13</sup>Then he said to the man, 'Stretch out your hand.' He stretched it out, and it was restored, as sound as the other. <sup>14</sup>But the Pharisees went out and conspired against him, how to destroy him.

# God's Chosen Servant

<sup>15</sup>When Jesus became aware of this, he departed. Many crowds followed him, and he cured all of them, <sup>16</sup>and he ordered them not to make him known. <sup>17</sup>This was to fulfil what had been spoken through the prophet Isaiah:
<sup>18</sup>'Here is my servant, whom I have chosen, my beloved, with whom my soul is well pleased. I will put my Spirit upon him, and he will proclaim justice to the Gentiles.

<sup>19</sup>He will not wrangle or cry aloud, nor will anyone hear his voice in the streets.
<sup>20</sup>He will not break a bruised reed or quench a smouldering wick until he brings justice to victory.
<sup>21</sup>And in his name the Gentiles will hope.'

## Jesus and Beelzebul

²²Then they brought to him a demoniac who was blind and mute; and he cured him, so that the one who had been mute could speak and see. ²³All the crowds were amazed and said, 'Can this be the Son of David?' ²⁴But when the Pharisees heard it, they said, 'It is only by Beelzebul, the ruler of the demons, that this fellow casts out the demons.' ²⁵He knew what they were thinking and said to them, 'Every kingdom divided against itself is laid waste, and no city or house divided against itself will stand. ²⁶If Satan casts out Satan, he is divided against himself; how then will his kingdom stand? ²⁷If I cast out demons by Beelzebul, by whom do your own exorcists cast them out? Therefore they will be your judges. ²⁸But if it is by the Spirit of God that I cast out demons, then the kingdom of God has come to you. ²⁹Or how can one enter a strong man's house and plunder his property, without first tying up the strong man? Then indeed the house can be plundered. ³⁰Whoever is not with me is against me, and whoever does not gather with me scatters. ³¹Therefore I tell you, people will be forgiven for every sin and blasphemy, but blasphemy against the Spirit will not be forgiven. ³²Whoever speaks a word against the Son of Man will be forgiven, but whoever speaks against the Holy Spirit will not be forgiven, either in this age or in the age to come.

## A Tree and Its Fruit

³³'Either make the tree good, and its fruit good; or make the tree bad, and its fruit bad; for the tree is known by its fruit. ³⁴You brood of vipers! How can you speak good things, when you are evil? For out of the abundance of the heart the mouth speaks. ³⁵The good person brings good things out of a good treasure, and the evil person brings evil things out of an evil treasure. ³⁶I tell you, on the day of judgement you will have to give an account for every careless word you utter; ³⁷for by your words you will be justified, and by your words you will be condemned.'

'... the kingdom of God has come to you.'

## The Sign of Jonah

<sup>38</sup>Then some of the scribes and Pharisees said to him, 'Teacher, we wish to see a sign from you.' <sup>39</sup>But he answered them, 'An evil and adulterous generation asks for a sign, but no sign will be given to it except the sign of the prophet Jonah. <sup>40</sup>For just as Jonah was three days and three nights in the belly of the sea monster, so for three days and three nights the Son of Man will be in the heart of the earth. <sup>41</sup>The people of Nineveh will rise up at the judgement with this generation and condemn it, because they repented at the proclamation of Jonah, and see, something greater than Jonah is here! <sup>42</sup>The queen of the South will rise up at the judgement with this generation and condemn it, because she came from the ends of the earth to listen to the wisdom of Solomon, and see, something greater than Solomon is here!

## The Return of the Unclean Spirit

<sup>43</sup>'When the unclean spirit has gone out of a person, it wanders through waterless regions looking for a resting place, but it finds none. <sup>44</sup>Then it says, 'I will return to my house from which I came.' When it comes, it finds it empty, swept, and put in order. <sup>45</sup>Then it goes and brings along seven other spirits more evil than itself, and they enter and live there; and the last state of that person is worse than the first. So will it be also with this evil generation.'

' ... so for three days and three nights the Son of Man will be in the heart of the earth.'

# The True Kindred of Jesus

[46]While he was still speaking to the crowds, his mother and his brothers were standing outside, wanting to speak to him. [47]Someone told him, 'Look, your mother and your brothers are standing outside, wanting to speak to you.' [48]But to the one who had told him this, Jesus replied, 'Who is my mother, and who are my brothers?' [49]And pointing to his disciples, he said, 'Here are my mother and my brothers! [50]For whoever does the will of my Father in heaven is my brother and sister and mother.'

## THE **PARABLES** OF JESUS (13:1–17:27)

**Jesus begins teaching in parables** to provide examples to his lessons.

### chapter THIRTEEN

## The Parable of the Sower

That same day Jesus went out of the house and sat beside the sea. ²Such great crowds gathered around him that he got into a boat and sat there, while the whole crowd stood on the beach. ³And he told them many things in parables, saying: 'Listen! A sower went out to sow. ⁴And as he sowed, some seeds fell on the path, and the birds came and ate them up. ⁵Other seeds fell on rocky ground, where they did not have much soil, and they sprang up quickly, since they had no depth of soil. ⁶But when the sun rose, they were scorched; and since they had no root, they withered away. ⁷Other seeds fell among thorns, and the thorns grew up and choked them. ⁸Other seeds fell on good soil and brought forth grain, some a hundredfold, some sixty, some thirty. ⁹Let anyone with ears listen!'

## The Purpose of the Parables

¹⁰Then the disciples came and asked him, 'Why do you speak to them in parables?' ¹¹He answered, 'To you it has been given to know the secrets of the kingdom of heaven, but to them it has not been given. ¹²For to those who have, more will be given, and they will have an abundance; but from those who have nothing, even what they have will be taken away. ¹³The reason I speak to them in parables is that "seeing they do not perceive, and hearing they do not listen, nor do they understand." ¹⁴With them indeed is fulfilled the prophecy of Isaiah that says:
"You will indeed listen, but never understand, and you will indeed look, but never perceive.
¹⁵For this people's heart has grown dull, and their ears are hard of hearing, and they have shut their eyes;
so that they might not look with their eyes, and listen with their ears,
and understand with their heart and turn – and I would heal them." ¹⁶But blessed are your eyes, for they see, and your ears, for they hear. ¹⁷Truly I tell you, many prophets and righteous people longed to see what you see, but did not see it, and to hear what you hear, but did not hear it.

## The Parable of the Sower **Explained**

[18]'Hear then the parable of the sower. [19]When anyone hears the word of the kingdom and does not understand it, the evil one comes and snatches away what is sown in the heart; this is what was sown on the path. [20]As for what was sown on rocky ground, this is the one who hears the word and immediately receives it with joy; [21]yet such a person has no root, but endures only for a while, and when trouble or persecution arises on account of the word, that person immediately falls away. [22]As for what was sown among thorns, this is the one who hears the word, but the cares of the world and the lure of wealth choke the word, and it yields nothing. [23]But as for what was sown on good soil, this is the one who hears the word and understands it, who indeed bears fruit and yields, in one case a hundredfold, in another sixty, and in another thirty.'

## The Parable of **Weeds among the Wheat**

[24]He put before them another parable: 'The kingdom of heaven may be compared to someone who sowed good seed in his field; [25]but while everybody was asleep, an enemy came and sowed weeds among the wheat, and then went away. [26]So when the plants came up and bore grain, then the weeds appeared as well. [27]And the slaves of the householder came and said to him, "Master, did you not sow good seed in your field? Where, then, did these weeds come from?" [28]He answered, "An enemy has done this." The slaves said to him, "Then do you want us to go and gather them?" [29]But he replied, "No; for in gathering the weeds you would uproot the wheat along with them. [30]Let both of them grow together until the harvest; and at harvest time I will tell the reapers, Collect the weeds first and bind them in bundles to be burned, but gather the wheat into my barn."'

# The Parable of the **Mustard Seed**

<sup>31</sup>He put before them another parable: 'The kingdom of heaven is like a mustard seed that someone took and sowed in his field; <sup>32</sup>it is the smallest of all the seeds, but when it has grown it is the greatest of shrubs and becomes a tree, so that the birds of the air come and make nests in its branches.'

# The Parable of the **Yeast**

<sup>33</sup>He told them another parable: 'The kingdom of heaven is like yeast that a woman took and mixed in with three measures of flour until all of it was leavened.'

# The **Use of Parables**

<sup>34</sup>Jesus told the crowds all these things in parables; without a parable he told them nothing. <sup>35</sup>This was to fulfil what had been spoken through the prophet:
'I will open my mouth to speak in parables;
I will proclaim what has been hidden from the foundation of the world.'

# **Jesus Explains** the Parable of the Weeds

<sup>36</sup>Then he left the crowds and went into the house. And his disciples approached him, saying, 'Explain to us the parable of the weeds of the field.' <sup>37</sup>He answered, 'The one who sows the good seed is the Son of Man; <sup>38</sup>the field is the world, and the good seed are the children of the kingdom; the weeds are the children of the evil one, <sup>39</sup>and the enemy who sowed them is the devil; the harvest is the end of the age, and the reapers are angels. <sup>40</sup>Just as the weeds are collected and burned up with fire, so will it be at the end of the age. <sup>41</sup>The Son of Man will send his angels, and they will collect out of his kingdom all causes of sin and all evildoers, <sup>42</sup>and they will throw them into the furnace of fire, where there will be weeping and gnashing of teeth. <sup>43</sup>Then the righteous will shine like the sun in the kingdom of their Father. Let anyone with ears listen!

# Three Parables

44'The kingdom of heaven is like treasure hidden in a field, which someone found and hid; then in his joy he goes and sells all that he has and buys that field. 45'Again, the kingdom of heaven is like a merchant in search of fine pearls; 46on finding one pearl of great value, he went and sold all that he had and bought it. 47'Again, the kingdom of heaven is like a net that was thrown into the sea and caught fish of every kind; 48when it was full, they drew it ashore, sat down, and put the good into baskets but threw out the bad. 49So it will be

at the end of the age. The angels will come out and separate the evil from the righteous 50and throw them into the furnace of fire, where there will be weeping and gnashing of teeth.

## Treasures New and Old

51"Have you understood all this?' They answered, 'Yes.' 52And he said to them, 'Therefore every scribe who has been trained for the kingdom of heaven is like the master of a household who brings out of his treasure what is new and what is old.'
53When Jesus had finished these parables, he left that place.

# The **Rejection** of Jesus at Nazareth

⁵⁴He came to his hometown and began to teach the people in their synagogue, so that they were astounded and said, 'Where did this man get this wisdom and these deeds of power? ⁵⁵Is not this the carpenter's son? Is not his mother called Mary? And are not his brothers James and Joseph and Simon and Judas? ⁵⁶And are not all his sisters with us? Where then did this man get all this?' ⁵⁷And they took offence at him. But Jesus said to them, 'Prophets are not without honour except in their own country and in their own house.' ⁵⁸And he did not do many deeds of power there, because of their unbelief.

'Where did this man get this wisdom and these deeds of power?'

5,000!

# chapter FOURTEEN

## The Death of John the Baptist

At that time Herod the ruler heard reports about Jesus; [2]and he said to his servants, 'This is John the Baptist; he has been raised from the dead, and for this reason these powers are at work in him.' [3]For Herod had arrested John, bound him, and put him in prison on account of Herodias, his brother Philip's wife, [4]because John had been telling him, 'It is not lawful for you to have her.' [5]Though Herod wanted to put him to death, he feared the crowd, because they regarded him as a prophet.

[6]But when Herod's birthday came, the daughter of Herodias danced before the company, and she pleased Herod [7]so much that he promised on oath to grant her whatever she might ask. [8]Prompted by her mother, she said, 'Give me the head of John the Baptist here on a platter.' [9]The king was grieved, yet out of regard for his oaths and for the guests, he commanded it to be given; [10]he sent and had John beheaded in the prison. [11]The head was brought on a platter and given to the girl, who brought it to her mother. [12]His disciples came and took the body and buried it; then they went and told Jesus.

## Feeding the Five Thousand

[13]Now when Jesus heard this, he withdrew from there in a boat to a deserted place by himself. But when the crowds heard it, they followed him on foot from the towns. [14]When he went ashore, he saw a great crowd; and he had compassion for them and cured their sick. [15]When it was evening, the disciples came to him and said, 'This is a deserted place, and the hour is now late; send the crowds away so that they may go into the villages and buy food for themselves.' [16]Jesus said to them, 'They need not go away; you give them something to eat.' [17]They replied, 'We have nothing here but five loaves and two fish.' [18]And he said, 'Bring them

here to me.' [19]Then he ordered the crowds to sit down on the grass. Taking the five loaves and the two fish, he looked up to heaven, and blessed and broke the loaves, and gave them to the disciples, and the disciples gave them to the crowds. [20]And all ate and were filled; and they took up what was left over of the broken pieces, twelve baskets full. [21]And those who ate were about five thousand men, besides women and children.

## Jesus Walks on the Water

[22]Immediately he made the disciples get into the boat and go on ahead to the other side, while he dismissed the crowds. [23]And after he had dismissed the crowds, he went up the mountain by himself to pray. When evening came, he was there alone, [24]but by this time the boat, battered by the waves, was far from the land, for the wind was against them. [25]And early in the morning he came walking toward them on the sea. [26]But when the disciples saw him walking on the sea, they were terrified, saying, 'It is a ghost!' And they cried out in fear. [27]But immediately Jesus spoke to them and said, 'Take heart, it is I; do not be afraid.'
[28]Peter answered him, 'Lord, if it is you, command me to come to you on the water.' [29]He said, 'Come.' So Peter got out of the boat, started walking on the water, and came toward Jesus. [30]But when he noticed the strong wind, he became frightened, and beginning to sink, he cried out, 'Lord, save me!' [31]Jesus immediately reached out his hand and caught him, saying to him, 'You of little faith, why did you doubt?' [32]When they got into the boat, the wind ceased. [33]And those in the boat worshipped him, saying, 'Truly you are the Son of God.'

Lluís Borrassà · St. Peter is Walking on the Water · 1411–1413

# Jesus Heals the Sick in Gennesaret

34When they had crossed over, they came to land at Gennesaret. 35After the people of that place recognised him, they sent word throughout the region and brought all who were sick to him, 36and begged him that they might touch even the fringe of his cloak; and all who touched it were healed.

## chapter FIFTEEN

# The Tradition of the Elders

Then Pharisees and scribes came to Jesus from Jerusalem and said, 2'Why do your disciples break the tradition of the elders? For they do not wash their hands before they eat.' 3He answered them, 'And why do you break the commandment of God for the sake of your tradition? 4For God said, "Honour your father and your mother," and, "Whoever speaks evil of father or mother must surely die." 5But you say that whoever tells father or mother, "Whatever support you might have had from me is given to God," then that person need not honour the father. 6So, for the sake of your tradition, you make void the word of God. 7You hypocrites! Isaiah prophesied rightly about you when he said:
8"This people honours me with their lips,
   but their hearts are far from me;
   9in vain do they worship me,
   teaching human precepts as doctrines.'"

James Tissot (French, 1836–1902) · The Pharisees and the Herodians Conspire Against Jesus (Les pharisiens et les hérodiens conspirent contre Jésus) · 1886–1894. *Opaque watercolor over graphite on grey wove paper, Image: 6 3/4 x 8 15/16 in. (17.1 x 22.7 cm). Brooklyn Museum, Purchased by public subscription, 00.159.97*

# Things That Defile

10Then he called the crowd to him and said to them, 'Listen and understand: 11it is not what goes into the mouth that defiles a person, but it is what comes out of the mouth that defiles.' 12Then the disciples approached and said to him, 'Do you know that the Pharisees took offence when they heard what you said?' 13He answered, 'Every plant that my heavenly Father has not planted will be uprooted. 14Let them alone; they are blind guides of the blind. And if one blind person guides another, both will fall into a pit.' 15But Peter said to him, 'Explain this parable to us.' 16Then he said, 'Are you also still without understanding? 17Do you not see that whatever goes into the mouth enters the stomach, and goes out into the sewer? 18But what comes out of the mouth proceeds from the heart, and this is what defiles. 19For out of the heart come evil intentions, murder, adultery, fornication, theft, false witness, slander. 20These are what defile a person, but to eat with unwashed hands does not defile.'

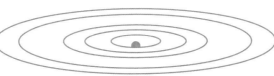

Jean Colombe · Christ and the Canaanite Woman · c. 1410

# The Canaanite Woman's Faith

²¹Jesus left that place and went away to the district of Tyre and Sidon. ²²Just then a Canaanite woman from that region came out and started shouting, 'Have mercy on me, Lord, Son of David; my daughter is tormented by a demon.' ²³But he did not answer her at all. And his disciples came and urged him, saying, 'Send her away, for she keeps shouting after us.' ²⁴He answered, 'I was sent only to the lost sheep of the house of Israel.' ²⁵But she came and knelt before him, saying, 'Lord, help me.' ²⁶He answered, 'It is not fair to take the children's food and throw it to the dogs.' ²⁷She said, 'Yes, Lord, yet even the dogs eat the crumbs that fall from their masters' table.' ²⁸Then Jesus answered her, 'Woman, great is your faith! Let it be done for you as you wish.' And her daughter was healed instantly.

# Jesus Cures Many People

²⁹After Jesus had left that place, he passed along the Sea of Galilee, and he went up the mountain, where he sat down. ³⁰Great crowds came to him, bringing with them the lame, the maimed, the blind, the mute, and many others. They put them at his feet, and he cured them, ³¹so that the crowd was amazed when they saw the mute speaking, the maimed whole, the lame walking, and the blind seeing. And they praised the God of Israel.

James Tissot (French, 1836–1902) · Jesus Heals the Blind and Lame on the Mountain (Sur la montagne Jésus guérit les aveugles et les boiteux) · 1886–1896. *Opaque watercolor over graphite on gray wove paper, Image: 6 3/4 x 9 3/16 in. (17.1 x 23.3 cm). Brooklyn Museum, Purchased by public subscription, 00.159.88*

# Feeding the Four Thousand

³²Then Jesus called his disciples to him and said, 'I have compassion for the crowd, because they have been with me now for three days and have nothing to eat; and I do not want to send them away hungry, for they might faint on the way.' ³³The disciples said to him, 'Where are we to get enough bread in the desert to feed so great a crowd?' ³⁴Jesus asked them, 'How many loaves have you?' They said, 'Seven, and a few small fish.' ³⁵Then ordering the crowd to sit down on the ground, ³⁶he took the seven loaves and the fish; and after giving thanks he broke them and gave them to the disciples, and the disciples gave them to the crowds. ³⁷And all of them ate and were filled; and they took up the broken pieces left over, seven baskets full. ³⁸Those who had eaten were four thousand men, besides women and children. ³⁹After sending away the crowds, he got into the boat and went to the region of Magadan.

# 4,000!

## chapter SIXTEEN

## The Demand for a Sign

The Pharisees and Sadducees came, and to test Jesus they asked him to show them a sign from heaven. [2]He answered them, 'When it is evening, you say, "It will be fair weather, for the sky is red." [3]And in the morning, "It will be stormy today, for the sky is red and threatening." You know how to interpret the appearance of the sky, but you cannot interpret the signs of the times. [4]An evil and adulterous generation asks for a sign, but no sign will be given to it except the sign of Jonah.' Then he left them and went away.

## The Yeast of the Pharisees and Sadducees

[5]When the disciples reached the other side, they had forgotten to bring any bread. [6]Jesus said to them, 'Watch out, and beware of the yeast of the Pharisees and Sadducees.' [7]They said to one another, 'It is because we have brought no bread.' [8]And becoming aware of it, Jesus said, 'You of little faith, why are you talking about having no bread? [9]Do you still not perceive? Do you not remember the five loaves for the five thousand, and how many baskets you gathered? [10]Or the seven loaves for the four thousand, and how many baskets you gathered? [11]How could you fail to perceive that I was not speaking about bread? Beware of the yeast of the Pharisees and Sadducees!' [12]Then they understood that he had not told them to beware of the yeast of bread, but of the teaching of the Pharisees and Sadducees.

## Peter's Declaration about Jesus

[13]Now when Jesus came into the district of Caesarea Philippi, he asked his disciples, 'Who do people say that the Son of Man is?' [14]And they said, 'Some say John the Baptist, but others Elijah, and still others Jeremiah or one of the prophets.' [15]He said to them, 'But who do you say that I am?' [16]Simon Peter answered, 'You are the Messiah, the Son of the living God.' [17]And Jesus answered him, 'Blessed are you, Simon son of Jonah! For flesh and blood has not revealed this to you, but my Father in heaven. [18]And I tell you, you are Peter, and on this rock I will build my church, and the gates of Hades will not prevail against it.

[19]I will give you the keys of the kingdom of heaven, and whatever you bind on earth will be bound in heaven, and whatever you loose on earth will be loosed in heaven.' [20]Then he sternly ordered the disciples not to tell anyone that he was the Messiah.

## Jesus Foretells His Death and Resurrection

[21]From that time on, Jesus began to show his disciples that he must go to Jerusalem and undergo great suffering at the hands of the elders and chief priests and scribes, and be killed, and on the third day be raised. [22]And Peter took him aside and began to rebuke him, saying, 'God forbid it, Lord! This must never happen to you.' [23]But he turned and said to Peter, 'Get behind me, Satan! You are a stumbling block to me; for you are setting your mind not on divine things but on human things.'

## The Cross and Self-Denial

[24]Then Jesus told his disciples, 'If any want to become my followers, let them deny themselves and take up their cross and follow me. [25]For those who want to save their life will lose it, and those who lose their life for my sake will find it. [26]For what will it profit them if they gain the whole world but forfeit their life? Or what will they give in return for their life?

[27]'For the Son of Man is to come with his angels in the glory of his Father, and then he will repay everyone for what has been done. [28]Truly I tell you, there are some standing here who will not taste death before they see the Son of Man coming in his kingdom.'

# chapter SEVENTEEN

# The Transfiguration

Six days later, Jesus took with him Peter and James and his brother John and led them up a high mountain, by themselves. ²And he was transfigured before them, and his face shone like the sun, and his clothes became dazzling white. ³Suddenly there appeared to them Moses and Elijah, talking with him. ⁴Then Peter said to Jesus, 'Lord, it is good for us to be here; if you wish, I will make three dwellings here, one for you, one for Moses, and one for Elijah.'

⁵While he was still speaking, suddenly a bright cloud overshadowed them, and from the cloud a voice said, 'This is my Son, the Beloved; with him I am well pleased; listen to him!' ⁶When the disciples heard this, they fell to the ground and were overcome by fear. ⁷But Jesus came and touched them, saying, 'Get up and do not be afraid.' ⁸And when they looked up, they saw no one except Jesus himself alone.

9As they were coming down the mountain, Jesus ordered them, 'Tell no one about the vision until after the Son of Man has been raised from the dead.' 10And the disciples asked him, 'Why, then, do the scribes say that Elijah must come first?' 11He replied, 'Elijah is indeed coming and will restore all things; 12but I tell you that Elijah has already come, and they did not recognise him, but they did to him whatever they pleased. So also the Son of Man is about to suffer at their hands.' 13Then the disciples understood that he was speaking to them about John the Baptist.

## Jesus Cures a Boy with a Demon

14When they came to the crowd, a man came to him, knelt before him, 15and said, 'Lord, have mercy on my son, for he is an epileptic and he suffers terribly; he often falls into the fire and often into the water. 16And I brought him to your disciples, but they could not cure him.' 17Jesus answered, 'You faithless and perverse generation, how much longer must I be with you? How much longer must I put up with you? Bring him here to me.' 18And Jesus rebuked the demon, and it came out of him, and the boy was cured instantly. 19Then the disciples came to Jesus privately and said, 'Why could we not cast it out?' 20He said to them, 'Because of your little faith. For truly I tell you, if you have faith the size of a mustard seed, you will say to this mountain, "Move from here to there," and it will move; and nothing will be impossible for you.'

## Jesus Again Foretells His Death and Resurrection

22As they were gathering in Galilee, Jesus said to them, 'The Son of Man is going to be betrayed into human hands, 23and they will kill him, and on the third day he will be raised.' And they were greatly distressed.

## Jesus and the Temple Tax

24When they reached Capernaum, the collectors of the temple tax came to Peter and said, 'Does your teacher not pay the temple tax?' 25He said, 'Yes, he does.' And when he came home, Jesus spoke of it first, asking, 'What do you think, Simon? From whom do kings of the earth take toll or tribute? From their children or from others?' 26When Peter said, 'From others,' Jesus said to him, 'Then the children are free. 27However, so that we do not give offence to them, go to the sea and cast a hook; take the first fish that comes up; and when you open its mouth, you will find a coin; take that and give it to them for you and me.'

Follower of Marinus van Reymerswaele · The Misers· 1458–1463

## FURTHER TEACHINGS OF JESUS (18:1–20:34)

**Jesus speaks** of **community** and **forgiveness**.

### chapter EIGHTEEN

# True Greatness

At that time the disciples came to Jesus and asked, 'Who is the greatest in the kingdom of heaven?' ²He called a child, whom he put among them, ³and said, 'Truly I tell you, unless you change and become like children, you will never enter the kingdom of heaven. ⁴Whoever becomes humble like this child is the greatest in the kingdom of heaven. ⁵Whoever welcomes one such child in my name welcomes me.

## Temptations to Sin

⁶'If any of you put a stumbling block before one of these little ones who believe in me, it would be better for you if a great millstone were fastened around your neck and you were drowned in the depth of the sea. ⁷Woe to the world because of stumbling blocks! Occasions for stumbling are bound to come, but woe to the one by whom the stumbling block comes!

⁸'If your hand or your foot causes you to stumble, cut it off and throw it away; it is better for you to enter life maimed or lame than to have two hands or two feet and to be thrown into the eternal fire. ⁹And if your eye causes you to stumble, tear it out and throw it away; it is better for you to enter life with one eye than to have two eyes and to be thrown into the hell of fire.

## The Parable of the Lost Sheep

¹⁰'Take care that you do not despise one of these little ones; for, I tell you, in heaven their angels continually see the face of my Father in heaven. ¹²What do you think? If a shepherd has a hundred sheep, and one of them has gone astray, does he not leave the ninety-nine on the mountains and go in search of the one that went astray? ¹³And if he finds it, truly I tell you, he rejoices over it more than over the ninety-nine that never went astray. ¹⁴So it is not the will of your Father in heaven that one of these little ones should be lost.

## Reproving Another Who Sins

¹⁵'If another member of the church sins against you, go and point out the fault when the two of you are alone. If the member listens to you, you have regained that one. ¹⁶But if you are not listened to, take one or two others along with you, so that every word may be confirmed by the evidence of two or three witnesses. ¹⁷If the member refuses to listen to them, tell it to the church; and if the offender refuses to listen even to the church, let such a one be to you as a Gentile and a tax collector. ¹⁸Truly I tell you, whatever you bind on earth will be bound in heaven, and whatever you loose on earth will be loosed in heaven. ¹⁹Again, truly I tell you, if two of you agree on earth about anything you ask, it will be done for you by my Father in heaven. ²⁰For where two or three are gathered in my name, I am there among them.'

'Truly I tell you, unless you change and become like children, you will never enter the kingdom of heaven.'

## Forgiveness

²¹Then Peter came and said to him, 'Lord, if another member of the church sins against me, how often should I forgive? As many as seven times?' ²²Jesus said to him, 'Not seven times, but, I tell you, seventy-seven times.

## The Parable of the
## Unforgiving Servant

²³'For this reason the kingdom of heaven may be compared to a king who wished to settle accounts with his slaves. ²⁴When he began the reckoning, one who owed him ten thousand talents was brought to him; ²⁵and, as he could not pay, his lord ordered him to be sold, together with his wife and children and all his possessions, and payment to be made. ²⁶So the slave fell on his knees before him, saying, "Have patience with me, and I will pay you everything." ²⁷And out of pity for him, the lord of that slave released him and forgave him the debt. ²⁸But that same slave, as he went out, came upon one of his fellow slaves who owed him a hundred denarii; and seizing him by the throat, he said, "Pay what you owe." ²⁹Then his fellow slave fell down and pleaded with him, "Have patience with me, and I will pay you." ³⁰But he refused; then he went and threw him into prison until he would pay the debt. ³¹When his fellow slaves saw what had happened, they were greatly distressed, and they went and reported to their lord all that had taken place. ³²Then his lord summoned him and said to him, "You wicked slave! I forgave you all that debt because you pleaded with me. ³³Should you not have had mercy on your fellow slave, as I had mercy on you?" ³⁴And in anger his lord handed him over to be tortured until he would pay his entire debt. ³⁵So my heavenly Father will also do to every one of you, if you do not forgive your brother or sister from your heart.'

## chapter NINETEEN

## Teaching about
## Divorce

When Jesus had finished saying these things, he left Galilee and went to the region of Judea beyond the Jordan. ²Large crowds followed him, and he cured them there.
³Some Pharisees came to him, and to test him they asked, 'Is it lawful for a man to divorce his wife for any cause?' ⁴He answered, 'Have you not read that the one who made them at the beginning "made them male and female," ⁵and said, "For this reason a man shall leave his father and mother and be joined to his wife, and the two shall become one flesh"? ⁶So they are no longer two, but one flesh. Therefore what God has joined together, let no one separate.' ⁷They said to him, 'Why then did Moses command us to give a certificate of dismissal and to divorce her?' ⁸He said to them, 'It was because you were so hard-hearted that Moses allowed you to divorce your wives, but from the beginning it was not so. ⁹And I say to you, whoever divorces his wife, except for unchastity, and marries another commits adultery.'

# Forgive

¹⁰His disciples said to him, 'If such is the case of a man with his wife, it is better not to marry.' ¹¹But he said to them, 'Not everyone can accept this teaching, but only those to whom it is given. ¹²For there are eunuchs who have been so from birth, and there are eunuchs who have been made eunuchs by others, and there are eunuchs who have made themselves eunuchs for the sake of the kingdom of heaven. Let anyone accept this who can.'

# Jesus Blesses Little Children

¹³Then little children were being brought to him in order that he might lay his hands on them and pray. The disciples spoke sternly to those who brought them; ¹⁴but Jesus said, 'Let the little children come to me, and do not stop them; for it is to such as these that the kingdom of heaven belongs.' ¹⁵And he laid his hands on them and went on his way.

# The Rich Young Man

¹⁶Then someone came to him and said, 'Teacher, what good deed must I do to have eternal life?' ¹⁷And he said to him, 'Why do you ask me about what is good? There is only one who is good. If you wish to enter into life, keep the commandments.' ¹⁸He said to him, 'Which ones?' And Jesus said, 'You shall not murder; You shall not commit adultery; You shall not steal; You shall not bear false witness; ¹⁹Honour your father and mother; also, You shall love your neighbour as yourself.' ²⁰The young man said to him, 'I have kept all these; what do I still lack?' ²¹Jesus said to him, 'If you wish to be perfect, go, sell your possessions, and give the money to the poor, and you will have treasure in heaven; then come, follow me.' ²²When the young man heard this word, he went away grieving, for he had many possessions. ²³Then Jesus said to his disciples, 'Truly I tell you, it will be hard for a rich person to enter the kingdom of heaven. ²⁴Again I tell you, it is easier for a camel to go through the eye of a needle than for someone who is rich to enter the kingdom of God.' ²⁵When the disciples heard this, they were greatly astounded and said, 'Then who can be saved?' ²⁶But Jesus looked at them and said, 'For mortals it is impossible, but for God all things are possible.' ²⁷Then Peter said in reply, 'Look, we have left everything and followed you. What then will we have?' ²⁸Jesus said to them, 'Truly I tell you, at the renewal of all things, when the Son of Man is seated on the throne of his glory, you who have followed me will also sit on twelve thrones, judging the twelve tribes of Israel. ²⁹And everyone who has left houses or brothers or sisters or father or mother or children or fields, for my name's sake, will receive a hundredfold, and will inherit eternal life. ³⁰But many who are first will be last, and the last will be first.

## chapter TWENTY

# The Labourers in the Vineyard

'For the kingdom of heaven is like a landowner who went out early in the morning to hire labourers for his vineyard. ²After agreeing with the labourers for the usual daily wage, he sent them into his vineyard. ³When he went out about nine o'clock, he saw others standing idle in the marketplace; ⁴and he said to them, "You also go into the vineyard, and I will pay you whatever is right." So they went. ⁵When he went out again about noon and about three o'clock, he did the same. ⁶And about five o'clock he went out and found others standing around; and he said to them, "Why are you standing here idle all day?" ⁷They said to him, "Because no one has hired us." He said to them, "You also go into the vineyard." ⁸When evening came, the owner of the vineyard said to his manager, "Call the labourers and give them their pay, beginning with the last and then going to the first." ⁹When those hired about five o'clock came, each of them received the usual daily wage. ¹⁰Now when the first came, they thought they would receive more; but each of them also received the usual daily wage. ¹¹And when they received it, they grumbled against the landowner, ¹²saying, "These last worked only one hour, and you have made them equal to us who have borne the burden of the day and the scorching heat." ¹³But he replied to one of them, "Friend, I am doing you no wrong; did you not agree with me for the usual daily wage? ¹⁴Take what belongs to you and go; I choose to give to this last the same as I give to you. ¹⁵Am I not allowed to do what I choose with what belongs to me? Or are you envious because I am generous?" ¹⁶So the last will be first, and the first will be last.'

# A Third Time Jesus Foretells His Death and Resurrection

¹⁷While Jesus was going up to Jerusalem, he took the twelve disciples aside by themselves, and said to them on the way, ¹⁸'See, we are going up to Jerusalem, and the Son of Man will be handed over to the chief priests and scribes, and they will condemn him to death; ¹⁹then they will hand him over to the Gentiles to be mocked and flogged and crucified; and on the third day he will be raised.'

## The Request of the Mother of James and John

²⁰Then the mother of the sons of Zebedee came to him with her sons, and kneeling before him, she asked a favour of him. ²¹And he said to her, 'What do you want?' She said to him, 'Declare that these two sons of mine will sit, one at your right hand and one at your left, in your kingdom.' ²²But Jesus answered, 'You do not know what you are asking. Are you able to drink the cup that I am about to drink?' They said to him, 'We are able.' ²³He said to them, 'You will indeed drink my cup, but to sit at my right hand and at my left, this is not mine to grant, but it is for those for whom it has been prepared by my Father.'

²⁴When the ten heard it, they were angry with the two brothers. ²⁵But Jesus called them to him and said, 'You know that the rulers of the Gentiles lord it over them, and their great ones are tyrants over them. ²⁶It will not be so among you; but whoever wishes to be great among you must be your servant, ²⁷and whoever wishes to be first among you must be your slave; ²⁸just as the Son of Man came not to be served but to serve, and to give his life a ransom for many.'

## Jesus Heals Two Blind Men

²⁹As they were leaving Jericho, a large crowd followed him. ³⁰There were two blind men sitting by the roadside. When they heard that Jesus was passing by, they shouted, 'Lord, have mercy on us, Son of David!' ³¹The crowd sternly ordered them to be quiet; but they shouted even more loudly, 'Have mercy on us, Lord, Son of David!' ³²Jesus stood still and called them, saying, 'What do you want me to do for you?' ³³They said to him, 'Lord, let our eyes be opened.' ³⁴Moved with compassion, Jesus touched their eyes. Immediately they regained their sight and followed him.

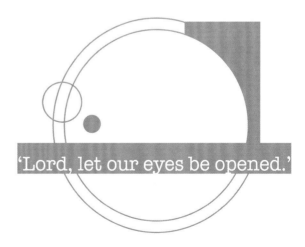

'Lord, let our eyes be opened.'

## JESUS' ARRIVAL IN JERUSALEM
## (21:1–25:46)

**Jesus** makes a **triumphant arrival** in **Jerusalem** on the back of a donkey, **preaches** and warns of forthcoming woe.

## chapter TWENTY-ONE

# Jesus' Triumphal Entry into Jerusalem

When they had come near Jerusalem and had reached Bethphage, at the Mount of Olives, Jesus sent two disciples, ²saying to them, 'Go into the village ahead of you, and immediately you will find a donkey tied, and a colt with her; untie them and bring them to me. ³If anyone says anything to you, just say this, "The Lord needs them." And he will send them immediately.' ⁴This took place to fulfil what had been spoken through the prophet, saying,
⁵'Tell the daughter of Zion,
Look, your king is coming to you,
humble, and mounted on a donkey, and on a colt, the foal of a donkey.'
⁶The disciples went and did as Jesus had directed them; ⁷they brought the donkey and the colt, and put their cloaks on them, and he sat on them. ⁸A very large crowd spread their cloaks on the road, and others cut branches from the trees and spread them on the road. ⁹The crowds that went ahead of him and that followed were shouting,
'Hosanna to the Son of David!
Blessed is the one who comes in the name of the Lord!
Hosanna in the highest heaven!' ¹⁰When he entered Jerusalem, the whole city was in turmoil, asking, 'Who is this?' ¹¹The crowds were saying, 'This is the prophet Jesus from Nazareth in Galilee.'

# Hosanna!
'Hosanna in the highest heaven!'

# Jesus Cleanses the Temple

¹²Then Jesus entered the temple and drove out all who were selling and buying in the temple, and he overturned the tables of the money changers and the seats of those who sold doves. ¹³He said to them, 'It is written,
"My house shall be called a house of prayer";
but you are making it a den of robbers.'
¹⁴The blind and the lame came to him in the temple, and he cured them. ¹⁵But when the chief priests and the scribes saw the amazing things that he did, and heard the children crying out in the temple, 'Hosanna to the Son of David,' they became angry ¹⁶and said to him, 'Do you hear what these are saying?' Jesus said to them, 'Yes; have you never read,
"Out of the mouths of infants and nursing babies
you have prepared praise for yourself"?'
¹⁷He left them, went out of the city to Bethany, and spent the night there.

## Jesus Curses the Fig Tree

[18]In the morning, when he returned to the city, he was hungry. [19]And seeing a fig tree by the side of the road, he went to it and found nothing at all on it but leaves. Then he said to it, 'May no fruit ever come from you again!' And the fig tree withered at once. [20]When the disciples saw it, they were amazed, saying, 'How did the fig tree wither at once?' [21]Jesus answered them, 'Truly I tell you, if you have faith and do not doubt, not only will you do what has been done to the fig tree, but even if you say to this mountain, "Be lifted up and thrown into the sea," it will be done. [22]Whatever you ask for in prayer with faith, you will receive.'

## The Authority of Jesus Questioned

[23]When he entered the temple, the chief priests and the elders of the people came to him as he was teaching, and said, 'By what authority are you doing these things, and who gave you this authority?' [24]Jesus said to them, 'I will also ask you one question; if you tell me the answer, then I will also tell you by what authority I do these things. [25]Did the baptism of John come from heaven, or was it of human origin?' And they argued with one another, 'If we say, "From heaven," he will say to us, "Why then did you not believe him?" [26]But if we say, "Of human origin," we are afraid of the crowd; for all regard John as a prophet.' [27]So they answered Jesus, 'We do not know.' And he said to them, 'Neither will I tell you by what authority I am doing these things.'

'Whatever you ask for in prayer with faith, you will receive.'

# The Parable of the
## Two Sons

<sup>28</sup>'What do you think? A man had two sons; he went to the first and said, "Son, go and work in the vineyard today." <sup>29</sup>He answered, "I will not"; but later he changed his mind and went. <sup>30</sup>The father went to the second and said the same; and he answered, "I go, sir"; but he did not go. <sup>31</sup>Which of the two did the will of his father?' They said, 'The first.' Jesus said to them, 'Truly I tell you, the tax collectors and the prostitutes are going into the kingdom of God ahead of you. <sup>32</sup>For John came to you in the way of righteousness and you did not believe him, but the tax collectors and the prostitutes believed him; and even after you saw it, you did not change your minds and believe him.

# The Parable of the
## Wicked Tenants

<sup>33</sup>'Listen to another parable. There was a landowner who planted a vineyard, put a fence around it, dug a wine press in it, and built a watchtower. Then he leased it to tenants and went to another country. <sup>34</sup>When the harvest time had come, he sent his slaves to the tenants to collect his produce. <sup>35</sup>But the tenants seized his slaves and beat one, killed another, and stoned another. <sup>36</sup>Again he sent other slaves, more than the first; and they treated them in the same way. <sup>37</sup>Finally he sent his son to them, saying, "They will respect my son." <sup>38</sup>But when the tenants saw the son, they said to themselves, "This is the heir; come, let us kill him and get his inheritance." <sup>39</sup>So they seized him, threw him out of the vineyard, and killed him. <sup>40</sup>Now when the owner of the vineyard comes, what will he do to those tenants?' <sup>41</sup>They said to him, 'He will put those wretches to a miserable death, and lease the vineyard to other tenants who will give him the produce at the harvest time.' <sup>42</sup>Jesus said to them, 'Have you never read in the scriptures:
"The stone that the builders rejected has become the cornerstone; this was the Lord's doing, and it is amazing in our eyes"? <sup>43</sup>Therefore I tell you, the kingdom of God will be taken away from you and given to a people that produces the fruits of the kingdom. <sup>44</sup>The one who falls on this stone will be broken to pieces; and it will crush anyone on whom it falls.' <sup>45</sup>When the chief priests and the Pharisees heard his parables, they realised that he was speaking about them. <sup>46</sup>They wanted to arrest him, but they feared the crowds, because they regarded him as a prophet.

## chapter TWENTY-TWO

# The Parable of the
## Wedding Banquet

Once more Jesus spoke to them in parables, saying: <sup>2</sup>'The kingdom of heaven may be compared to a king who gave a wedding banquet for his son. <sup>3</sup>He sent his slaves to call those who had been invited to the wedding banquet, but they would not come. <sup>4</sup>Again he sent other slaves, saying, "Tell those who have been invited: Look, I have prepared my dinner, my oxen and my fat calves have been slaughtered, and everything is ready; come to the wedding banquet." <sup>5</sup>But they made light of it and went away, one to his farm, another to his business, <sup>6</sup>while the rest seized his slaves, mistreated them, and killed them. <sup>7</sup>The king was

'Give therefore to the emperor the things that are the emperor's, and to God the things that are God's.'

## The Question about Paying Taxes

¹⁵Then the Pharisees went and plotted to entrap him in what he said. ¹⁶So they sent their disciples to him, along with the Herodians, saying, 'Teacher, we know that you are sincere, and teach the way of God in accordance with truth, and show deference to no one; for you do not regard people with partiality. ¹⁷Tell us, then, what you think. Is it lawful to pay taxes to the emperor, or not?' ¹⁸But Jesus, aware of their malice, said, 'Why are you putting me to the test, you hypocrites? ¹⁹Show me the coin used for the tax.' And they brought him a denarius. ²⁰Then he said to them, 'Whose head is this, and whose title?' ²¹They answered, 'The emperor's.' Then he said to them, 'Give therefore to the emperor the things that are the emperor's, and to God the things that are God's.' ²²When they heard this, they were amazed; and they left him and went away.

## The Question about the Resurrection

²³The same day some Sadducees came to him, saying there is no resurrection; and they asked him a question, saying, ²⁴'Teacher, Moses said, "If a man dies childless, his brother shall marry the widow, and raise up children for his brother." ²⁵Now there were seven brothers among us; the first married, and died childless, leaving the widow to his brother. ²⁶The second did the same, so also the third, down to the seventh. ²⁷Last of all, the woman herself died. ²⁸In the resurrection, then, whose wife of the seven will she be? For all of them had married her.'

²⁹Jesus answered them, 'You are wrong, because you know neither the scriptures nor the power of God. ³⁰For in the resurrection they neither marry nor are given in marriage, but are like angels in

enraged. He sent his troops, destroyed those murderers, and burned their city. ⁸Then he said to his slaves, "The wedding is ready, but those invited were not worthy. ⁹Go therefore into the main streets, and invite everyone you find to the wedding banquet." ¹⁰Those slaves went out into the streets and gathered all whom they found, both good and bad; so the wedding hall was filled with guests.

¹¹'But when the king came in to see the guests, he noticed a man there who was not wearing a wedding robe, ¹²and he said to him, "Friend, how did you get in here without a wedding robe?" And he was speechless. ¹³Then the king said to the attendants, "Bind him hand and foot, and throw him into the outer darkness, where there will be weeping and gnashing of teeth." ¹⁴For many are called, but few are chosen.'

heaven. ³¹And as for the resurrection of the dead, have you not read what was said to you by God, ³²"I am the God of Abraham, the God of Isaac, and the God of Jacob"? He is God not of the dead, but of the living.' ³³And when the crowd heard it, they were astounded at his teaching.

## The Greatest Commandment

³⁴When the Pharisees heard that he had silenced the Sadducees, they gathered together, ³⁵and one of them, a lawyer, asked him a question to test him. ³⁶'Teacher, which commandment in the law is the greatest?' ³⁷He said to him, '"You shall love the Lord your God with all your heart, and with all your soul, and with all your mind." ³⁸This is the greatest and first commandment. ³⁹And a second is like it: "You shall love your neighbour as yourself." ⁴⁰On these two commandments hang all the law and the prophets.'

## The Question about David's Son

⁴¹Now while the Pharisees were gathered together, Jesus asked them this question: ⁴²'What do you think of the Messiah? Whose son is he?' They said to him, 'The son of David.' ⁴³He said to them, 'How is it then that David by the Spirit calls him Lord, saying,
⁴⁴"The Lord said to my Lord,
'Sit at my right hand,
until I put your enemies under your feet'"?
⁴⁵If David thus calls him Lord, how can he be his son?' ⁴⁶No one was able to give him an answer, nor from that day did anyone dare to ask him any more questions.

## chapter TWENTY-THREE

## Jesus Denounces Scribes and Pharisees

Then Jesus said to the crowds and to his disciples, ²'The scribes and the Pharisees sit on Moses' seat; ³therefore, do whatever they teach you and follow it; but do not do as they do, for they do not practice what they teach. ⁴They tie up heavy burdens, hard to bear, and lay them on the shoulders of others; but they themselves are unwilling to lift a finger to move them. ⁵They do all their deeds to be seen by others; for they make their phylacteries broad and their fringes long. ⁶They love to have the place of honour at banquets and the best seats in the synagogues, ⁷and to be greeted with respect in the marketplaces, and to have people

call them rabbi. ⁸But you are not to be called rabbi, for you have one teacher, and you are all students. ⁹And call no one your father on earth, for you have one Father – the one in heaven. ¹⁰Nor are you to be called instructors, for you have one instructor, the Messiah. ¹¹The greatest among you will be your servant. ¹²All who exalt themselves will be humbled, and all who humble themselves will be exalted.

¹³'But woe to you, scribes and Pharisees, hypocrites! For you lock people out of the kingdom of heaven. For you do not go in yourselves, and when others are going in, you stop them. ¹⁵Woe to you, scribes and Pharisees, hypocrites! For you cross sea and land to make a single convert, and you make the new convert twice as much a child of hell as yourselves. ¹⁶'Woe to you, blind guides, who say, "Whoever swears by the sanctuary is bound by nothing,

but whoever swears by the gold of the sanctuary is bound by the oath." ¹⁷You blind fools! For which is greater, the gold or the sanctuary that has made the gold sacred? ¹⁸And you say, 'Whoever swears by the altar is bound by nothing, but whoever swears by the gift that is on the altar is bound by the oath.' ¹⁹How blind you are! For which is greater, the gift or the altar that makes the gift sacred? ²⁰So whoever swears by the altar, swears by it and by everything on it; ²¹and whoever swears by the sanctuary, swears by it and by the one who dwells in it; ²²and whoever swears by heaven, swears by the throne of God and by the one who is seated upon it.

²³'Woe to you, scribes and Pharisees, hypocrites! For you tithe mint, dill, and cummin, and have neglected the weightier matters of the law: justice and mercy and faith.

# Woe!

who murdered the prophets. ³²Fill up, then, the measure of your ancestors. ³³You snakes, you brood of vipers! How can you escape being sentenced to hell? ³⁴Therefore I send you prophets, sages, and scribes, some of whom you will kill and crucify, and some you will flog in your synagogues and pursue from town to town, ³⁵so that upon you may come all the righteous blood shed on earth, from the blood of righteous Abel to the blood of Zechariah son of Barachiah, whom you murdered between the sanctuary and the altar. ³⁶Truly I tell you, all this will come upon this generation.

## The Lament over Jerusalem

³⁷'Jerusalem, Jerusalem, the city that kills the prophets and stones those who are sent to it! How often have I desired to gather your children together as a hen gathers her brood under her wings, and you were not willing! ³⁸See, your house is left to you, desolate. ³⁹For I tell you, you will not see me again until you say, "Blessed is the one who comes in the name of the Lord."'

It is these you ought to have practiced without neglecting the others. ²⁴You blind guides! You strain out a gnat but swallow a camel!
²⁵'Woe to you, scribes and Pharisees, hypocrites! For you clean the outside of the cup and of the plate, but inside they are full of greed and self-indulgence. ²⁶You blind Pharisee! First clean the inside of the cup, so that the outside also may become clean.
²⁷'Woe to you, scribes and Pharisees, hypocrites! For you are like whitewashed tombs, which on the outside look beautiful, but inside they are full of the bones of the dead and of all kinds of filth. ²⁸So you also on the outside look righteous to others, but inside you are full of hypocrisy and lawlessness.
²⁹'Woe to you, scribes and Pharisees, hypocrites! For you build the tombs of the prophets and decorate the graves of the righteous, ³⁰and you say, "If we had lived in the days of our ancestors, we would not have taken part with them in shedding the blood of the prophets." ³¹Thus you testify against yourselves that you are descendants of those

## chapter TWENTY-FOUR

## The **Destruction** of the **Temple** Foretold

As Jesus came out of the temple and was going away, his disciples came to point out to him the buildings of the temple. ²Then he asked them, 'You see all these, do you not? Truly I tell you, not one stone will be left here upon another; all will be thrown down.'

## Signs of the **End of the Age**

³When he was sitting on the Mount of Olives, the disciples came to him privately, saying, 'Tell us, when will this be, and what will be the sign of your coming and of the end of the age?' ⁴Jesus answered them, 'Beware that no one leads you astray. ⁵For many will come in my name, saying, 'I am the Messiah!' and they will lead many astray. ⁶And you will hear of wars and rumours of wars; see that you are not alarmed; for this must take place, but the end is not yet. ⁷For nation will rise against nation, and kingdom against kingdom, and there will be famines and earthquakes in various places: ⁸all this is but the beginning of the birth pangs.

## **Persecutions** Foretold

⁹'Then they will hand you over to be tortured and will put you to death, and you will be hated by all nations because of my name. ¹⁰Then many will fall away, and they will betray one another and hate one another. ¹¹And many false prophets will arise and lead many astray. ¹²And because of the increase of lawlessness, the love of many will grow cold. ¹³But the one who endures to the end will be saved. ¹⁴And this good news of the kingdom will be proclaimed throughout the world, as a testimony to all the nations; and then the end will come.

## The Desolating **Sacrilege**

¹⁵'So when you see the desolating sacrilege standing in the holy place, as was spoken of by the prophet Daniel (let the reader understand), ¹⁶then those in Judea must flee to the mountains; ¹⁷the one on the housetop must not go down to take what is in the house; ¹⁸the one in the field must not turn back to get a coat. ¹⁹Woe to those who are pregnant and to

' ... they will see "the Son of Man coming on the clouds of heaven". '

those who are nursing infants in those days! ²⁰Pray that your flight may not be in winter or on a sabbath. ²¹For at that time there will be great suffering, such as has not been from the beginning of the world until now, no, and never will be. ²²And if those days had not been cut short, no one would be saved; but for the sake of the elect those days will be cut short. ²³Then if anyone says to you, "Look! Here is the Messiah!" or "There he is!" – do not believe it. ²⁴For false messiahs and false prophets will appear and produce great signs and omens, to lead astray, if possible, even the elect. ²⁵Take note, I have told you beforehand. ²⁶So, if they say to you, "Look! He is in the wilderness," do not go out. If they say, "Look! He is in the inner rooms," do not believe it. ²⁷For as the lightning comes from the east and flashes as far as the west, so will be the coming of the Son of Man. ²⁸Wherever the corpse is, there the vultures will gather.

## The Coming of the Son of Man

²⁹'Immediately after the suffering of those days
the sun will be darkened,
and the moon will not give its light;
the stars will fall from heaven,
and the powers of heaven will be shaken.
³⁰Then the sign of the Son of Man will appear in heaven, and then all the tribes of the earth will mourn, and they will see "the Son of Man coming on the clouds of heaven" with power and great glory. ³¹And he will send out his angels with a loud trumpet call, and they will gather his elect from the four winds, from one end of heaven to the other.

## The Lesson of the Fig Tree

³²"From the fig tree learn its lesson: as soon as its branch becomes tender and puts forth its leaves, you know that summer is near. ³³So also, when you see all these things, you know that he is near, at the very gates. ³⁴Truly I tell you, this generation will not pass away until all these things have taken place. ³⁵Heaven and earth will pass away, but my words will not pass away.

## The Necessity for Watchfulness

³⁶"But about that day and hour no one knows, neither the angels of heaven, nor the Son, but only the Father. ³⁷For as the days of Noah were, so will be the coming of the Son of Man. ³⁸For as in those days before the flood they were eating and drinking, marrying and giving in marriage, until the day Noah entered the ark, ³⁹and they knew nothing until the flood came and swept them all away, so too will be the coming of the Son of Man. ⁴⁰Then two will be in the field; one will be taken and one will be left. ⁴¹Two women will be grinding meal together; one will be taken and one will be left. ⁴²Keep awake therefore, for you do not know on what day your Lord is coming. ⁴³But understand this: if the owner of the house had known in what part of the night the thief was coming, he would have stayed awake and would not have let his house be broken into. ⁴⁴Therefore you also must be ready, for the Son of Man is coming at an unexpected hour.

## The Faithful or the Unfaithful Slave

⁴⁵"Who then is the faithful and wise slave, whom his master has put in charge of his household, to give the other slaves their allowance of food at the proper time? ⁴⁶Blessed is that slave whom his master will find at work when he arrives. ⁴⁷Truly I tell you, he will put that one in charge of all his possessions. ⁴⁸But if that wicked slave says to himself, "My master is delayed," ⁴⁹and he begins to beat his fellow slaves, and eats and drinks with drunkards, ⁵⁰the master of that slave will come on a day when he does not expect him and at an hour that he does not know. ⁵¹He will cut him in pieces and put him with the hypocrites, where there will be weeping and gnashing of teeth.

## chapter TWENTY-FIVE

## The Parable of the Ten Bridesmaids

'Then the kingdom of heaven will be like this. Ten bridesmaids took their lamps and went to meet the bridegroom. ²Five of them were foolish, and five were wise. ³When the foolish took their lamps, they took no oil with them; ⁴but the wise took flasks of oil with their lamps. ⁵As the bridegroom was delayed, all of them became drowsy and slept. ⁶But at midnight there was a shout, "Look! Here is the bridegroom! Come out to meet him." ⁷Then all those bridesmaids got up and trimmed their lamps. ⁸The foolish said to the wise, "Give us some of your oil, for our lamps are going out." ⁹But the wise replied, "No! there will not be enough for you and for us; you had better go to the dealers and buy some for yourselves."

**Matthew**

'Keep awake therefore, for you know neither the day nor the hour.'

¹⁰And while they went to buy it, the bridegroom came, and those who were ready went with him into the wedding banquet; and the door was shut. ¹¹Later the other bridesmaids came also, saying, 'Lord, lord, open to us.' ¹²But he replied, "Truly I tell you, I do not know you." ¹³Keep awake therefore, for you know neither the day nor the hour.

# The Parable of the
## Talents

¹⁴'For it is as if a man, going on a journey, summoned his slaves and entrusted his property to them; ¹⁵to one he gave five talents, to another two, to another one, to each according to his ability. Then he went away. ¹⁶The one who had received the five talents went off at once and traded with them, and made five more talents. ¹⁷In the same way, the one who had the two talents made two more talents. ¹⁸But the one who had received the one talent went off and dug a hole in the ground and hid his master's money. ¹⁹After a long time the master of those slaves came and settled accounts with them. ²⁰Then the one who had received the five talents came forward, bringing five more talents, saying, "Master, you handed over to me five talents; see, I have made five more talents." ²¹His master said to him, "Well done, good and trustworthy slave; you have been trustworthy in a few things, I will put you in charge of many things; enter into the joy of your master." ²²And the one with the two talents also came forward, saying, "Master, you handed over to me two talents; see, I have made two more talents." ²³His master said to him, "Well done, good and trustworthy slave;

you have been trustworthy in a few things, I will put you in charge of many things; enter into the joy of your master." 24Then the one who had received the one talent also came forward, saying, "Master, I knew that you were a harsh man, reaping where you did not sow, and gathering where you did not scatter seed; 25so I was afraid, and I went and hid your talent in the ground. Here you have what is yours." 26But his master replied, "You wicked and lazy slave! You knew, did you, that I reap where I did not sow, and gather where I did not scatter? 27Then you ought to have invested my money with the bankers, and on my return I would have received what was my own with interest. 28So take the talent from him, and give it to the one with the ten talents. 29For to all those who have, more will be given, and they will have an abundance; but from those who have nothing, even what they have will be taken away. 30As for this worthless slave, throw him into the outer darkness, where there will be weeping and gnashing of teeth."

# The Judgement of the Nations

31"When the Son of Man comes in his glory, and all the angels with him, then he will sit on the throne of his glory. 32All the nations will be gathered before him, and he will separate people one from another as a shepherd separates the sheep from the goats, 33and he will put the sheep at his right hand and the goats at the left. 34Then the king will say to those at his right hand, "Come, you that are blessed by my Father, inherit the kingdom prepared for you from the foundation of the world; 35for I was hungry and you gave me food, I was thirsty and you gave me something to drink, I was a stranger and you welcomed me, 36I was naked and you gave me clothing, I was sick and you took care of me, I was in prison and you visited me." 37Then the righteous will answer him, "Lord, when was it that we saw you hungry and gave you food, or thirsty and gave you something to drink? 38And when was it that we saw you a stranger and welcomed you, or naked and gave you clothing? 39And when was it that we saw you sick or in prison and visited you?" 40And the king will answer them, "Truly I tell you, just as you did it to one of the least of these who are members of my family, you did it to me." 41Then he will say to those at his left hand, "You that are accursed, depart from me into the eternal fire prepared for the devil and his angels; 42for I was hungry and you gave me no food, I was thirsty and you gave me nothing to drink, 43I was a stranger and you did not welcome me, naked and you did not give me clothing, sick and in prison and you did not visit me." 44Then they also will answer, "Lord, when was it that we saw you hungry or thirsty or a stranger or naked or sick or in prison, and did not take care of you?" 45Then he will answer them, "Truly I tell you, just as you did not do it to one of the least of these, you did not do it to me." 46And these will go away into eternal punishment, but the righteous into eternal life.'

'When the Son of Man comes in his glory, and all the angels with him, then he will sit on the throne of his glory.'

Jesus' **sacrifice** for all the **sin in the world**, by his **trial and crucifixion**.

## THE BETRAYAL, PASSION AND DEATH OF JESUS (26:1–28:20)

'What will you give me if I betray him to you?'
They paid him thirty pieces of silver.

## chapter TWENTY-SIX

# The Plot to Kill Jesus

When Jesus had finished saying all these things, he said to his disciples, [2]'You know that after two days the Passover is coming, and the Son of Man will be handed over to be crucified.' [3]Then the chief priests and the elders of the people gathered in the palace of the high priest, who was called Caiaphas, [4]and they conspired to arrest Jesus by stealth and kill him. [5]But they said, 'Not during the festival, or there may be a riot among the people.'

# The Anointing at Bethany

[6]Now while Jesus was at Bethany in the house of Simon the leper, [7]a woman came to him with an alabaster jar of very costly ointment, and she poured it on his head as he sat at the table. [8]But when the disciples saw it, they were angry and said, 'Why this waste? [9]For this ointment could have been sold for a large sum, and the money given to the poor.' [10]But Jesus, aware of this, said to them, 'Why do you trouble the woman? She has performed a good service for me. [11]For you always have the poor with you, but you will not always have me. [12]By pouring this ointment on my body she has prepared me for burial. [13]Truly I tell you, wherever this good news is proclaimed in the whole world, what she has done will be told in remembrance of her.'

## Judas Agrees to Betray Jesus

<sup>14</sup>Then one of the twelve, who was called Judas Iscariot, went to the chief priests <sup>15</sup>and said, 'What will you give me if I betray him to you?' They paid him thirty pieces of silver. <sup>16</sup>And from that moment he began to look for an opportunity to betray him.

## The Passover with the Disciples

<sup>17</sup>On the first day of Unleavened Bread the disciples came to Jesus, saying, 'Where do you want us to make the preparations for you to eat the Passover?' <sup>18</sup>He said, 'Go into the city to a certain man, and say to him, "The Teacher says, My time is near; I will keep the Passover at your house with my disciples."' <sup>19</sup>So the disciples did as Jesus had directed them, and they prepared the Passover meal.
<sup>20</sup>When it was evening, he took his place with the twelve; <sup>21</sup>and while they were eating, he said, 'Truly I tell you, one of you will betray me.' <sup>22</sup>And they became greatly distressed and began to say to him one after another, 'Surely not I, Lord?' <sup>23</sup>He answered, 'The one who has dipped his hand into the bowl with me will betray me. <sup>24</sup>The Son of Man goes as it is written of him, but woe to that one by whom the Son of Man is betrayed! It would have been better for that one not to have been born.' <sup>25</sup>Judas, who betrayed him, said, 'Surely not I, Rabbi?' He replied, 'You have said so.'

'Drink from it, all of you; for this is my blood of the covenant ...'

Simon Ushakov · The Last Supper · 1685

## The Institution of the Lord's Supper

<sup>26</sup>While they were eating, Jesus took a loaf of bread, and after blessing it he broke it, gave it to the disciples, and said, 'Take, eat; this is my body.' <sup>27</sup>Then he took a cup, and after giving thanks he gave it to them, saying, 'Drink from it, all of you; <sup>28</sup>for this is my blood of the covenant, which is poured out for many for the forgiveness of sins. <sup>29</sup>I tell you, I will never again drink of this fruit of the vine until that day when I drink it new with you in my Father's kingdom.'
<sup>30</sup>When they had sung the hymn, they went out to the Mount of Olives.

## Peter's Denial Foretold

<sup>31</sup>Then Jesus said to them, 'You will all become deserters because of me this night; for it is written,
"I will strike the shepherd,
and the sheep of the flock will be scattered."
<sup>32</sup>But after I am raised up, I will go ahead of you to Galilee.' <sup>33</sup>Peter said to him, 'Though all become deserters because of you, I will never desert you.'

[34]Jesus said to him, 'Truly I tell you, this very night, before the cock crows, you will deny me three times.' [35]Peter said to him, 'Even though I must die with you, I will not deny you.' And so said all the disciples.

# Jesus Prays in
## Gethsemane

[36]Then Jesus went with them to a place called Gethsemane; and he said to his disciples, 'Sit here while I go over there and pray.' [37]He took with him Peter and the two sons of Zebedee, and began to be grieved and agitated. [38]Then he said to them, 'I am deeply grieved, even to death; remain here, and stay awake with me.' [39]And going a little farther, he threw himself on the ground and prayed, 'My Father, if it is possible, let this cup pass from me; yet not what I want but what you want.' [40]Then he came to the disciples and found them sleeping; and he said to Peter, 'So, could you not stay awake with me one hour? [41]Stay awake and pray that you may not come into the time of trial; the spirit indeed is willing, but the flesh is weak.' [42]Again he went away for the second time and prayed, 'My Father, if this cannot pass unless I drink it, your will be done.' [43]Again he came and found them sleeping, for their eyes were heavy. [44]So leaving them again, he went away and prayed for the third time, saying the same words. [45]Then he came to the disciples and said to them, 'Are you still sleeping and taking your rest? See, the hour is at hand, and the Son of Man is betrayed into the hands of sinners. [46]Get up, let us be going. See, my betrayer is at hand.'

## The Betrayal and Arrest of Jesus

⁴⁷While he was still speaking, Judas, one of the twelve, arrived; with him was a large crowd with swords and clubs, from the chief priests and the elders of the people. ⁴⁸Now the betrayer had given them a sign, saying, 'The one I will kiss is the man; arrest him.' ⁴⁹At once he came up to Jesus and said, 'Greetings, Rabbi!' and kissed him. ⁵⁰Jesus said to him, 'Friend, do what you are here to do.' Then they came and laid hands on Jesus and arrested him. ⁵¹Suddenly, one of those with Jesus put his hand on his sword, drew it, and struck the slave of the high priest, cutting off his ear. ⁵²Then Jesus said to him, 'Put your sword back into its place; for all who take the sword will perish by the sword. ⁵³Do you think that I cannot appeal to my Father, and he will at once send me more than twelve legions of angels? ⁵⁴But how then would the scriptures be fulfilled, which say it must happen in this way?' ⁵⁵At that hour Jesus said to the crowds, 'Have you come out with swords and clubs to arrest me as though I were a bandit? Day after day I sat in the temple teaching, and you did not arrest me. ⁵⁶But all this has taken place, so that the scriptures of the prophets may be fulfilled.' Then all the disciples deserted him and fled.

> 'So, could you not stay awake with me one hour? ... the spirit is willing, but the flesh is weak.'

## Jesus before the High Priest

⁵⁷Those who had arrested Jesus took him to Caiaphas the high priest, in whose house the scribes and the elders had gathered. ⁵⁸But Peter was following him at a distance, as far as the courtyard of the high priest; and going inside, he sat with the guards in order to see how this would end. ⁵⁹Now the chief priests and the whole council were looking for false testimony against Jesus so that they might put him to death, ⁶⁰but they found none, though many false witnesses came forward. At last two came forward ⁶¹and said, 'This fellow said, "I am able to destroy the temple of God and to build it in three days."' ⁶²The high priest stood up and said, 'Have you no answer? What is it that they testify against you?' ⁶³But Jesus was silent. Then the high priest said to him, 'I put you under oath before the living God, tell us if you are the Messiah, the Son of God.' ⁶⁴Jesus said to him, 'You have said so. But I tell you,
From now on you will see the Son of Man seated at the right hand of Power
and coming on the clouds of heaven.'
⁶⁵Then the high priest tore his clothes and said, 'He has blasphemed! Why do we still need witnesses? You have now heard his blasphemy. ⁶⁶What is your verdict?' They answered, 'He deserves death.' ⁶⁷Then they spat in his face and struck him; and some slapped him, ⁶⁸saying, 'Prophesy to us, you Messiah! Who is it that struck you?'

# Peter's Denial of Jesus

69Now Peter was sitting outside in the courtyard. A servant-girl came to him and said, 'You also were with Jesus the Galilean.' 70But he denied it before all of them, saying, 'I do not know what you are talking about.' 71When he went out to the porch, another servant-girl saw him, and she said to the bystanders, 'This man was with Jesus of Nazareth.' 72Again he denied it with an oath, 'I do not know the man.' 73After a little while the bystanders came up and said to Peter, 'Certainly you are also one of them, for your accent betrays you.' 74Then he began to curse, and he swore an oath, 'I do not know the man!' At that moment the cock crowed. 75Then Peter remembered what Jesus had said: 'Before the cock crows, you will deny me three times.' And he went out and wept bitterly.

## chapter TWENTY-SEVEN

# Jesus Brought before **Pilate**

When morning came, all the chief priests and the elders of the people conferred together against Jesus in order to bring about his death. 2They bound him, led him away, and handed him over to Pilate the governor.

# The **Suicide of Judas**

3When Judas, his betrayer, saw that Jesus was condemned, he repented and brought back the thirty pieces of silver to the chief priests and the elders. 4He said, 'I have sinned by betraying innocent blood.' But they said, 'What is that to us? See to it yourself.' 5Throwing down the pieces of silver in the temple, he departed; and he went and hanged himself. 6But the chief priests, taking the pieces of silver, said, 'It is not lawful to put them into the treasury, since they are blood money.' ⁷After conferring together, they used them to buy the potter's field as a place to bury foreigners. ⁸For this reason that field has been called the Field of Blood to this day. ⁹Then was fulfilled what had been spoken through the prophet Jeremiah, 'And they took the thirty pieces of silver, the price of the one on whom a price had been set, on whom some of the people of Israel had set a price, ¹⁰and they gave them for the potter's field, as the Lord commanded me.'

# Pilate **Questions** Jesus

¹¹Now Jesus stood before the governor; and the governor asked him, 'Are you the King of the Jews?' Jesus said, 'You say so.' ¹²But when he was accused by the chief priests and elders, he did not answer. ¹³Then Pilate said to him, 'Do you not hear how many accusations they make against you?' ¹⁴But he gave him no answer, not even to a single charge, so that the governor was greatly amazed.

# **Barabbas** or **Jesus**?

¹⁵Now at the festival the governor was accustomed to release a prisoner for the crowd, anyone whom they wanted. ¹⁶At that time they had a notorious prisoner, called Jesus Barabbas. ¹⁷So after they had gathered, Pilate said to them, 'Whom do you want me to release for you, Jesus Barabbas or Jesus who is called the Messiah?' ¹⁸For he realised that it was out of jealousy that they had handed him over. ¹⁹While he was sitting on the judgement seat, his wife sent word to him, 'Have nothing to do with that innocent man, for today I have suffered a great deal because of a dream about him.' ²⁰Now the chief priests and the elders persuaded the crowds to ask for Barabbas and to have Jesus killed. ²¹The governor again said to them, 'Which of the two do you want me to release for you?' And they said, 'Barabbas.' ²²Pilate said to them, 'Then what should I do with Jesus who is called the Messiah?' All of them said, 'Let him be crucified!' ²³Then he asked, 'Why, what evil has he done?' But they shouted all the more, 'Let him be crucified!'

# Pilate Hands Jesus over to be **Crucified**

²⁴So when Pilate saw that he could do nothing, but rather that a riot was beginning, he took some water and washed his hands before the crowd, saying, 'I am innocent of this man's blood; see to it yourselves.' ²⁵Then the people as a whole answered, 'His blood be on us and on our children!'
²⁶So he released Barabbas for them; and after flogging Jesus, he handed him over to be crucified.

## The Soldiers Mock Jesus

²⁷Then the soldiers of the governor took Jesus into the governor's headquarters, and they gathered the whole cohort around him. ²⁸They stripped him and put a scarlet robe on him, ²⁹and after twisting some thorns into a crown, they put it on his head. They put a reed in his right hand and knelt before him and mocked him, saying, 'Hail, King of the Jews!' ³⁰They spat on him, and took the reed and struck him on the head. ³¹After mocking him, they stripped him of the robe and put his own clothes on him. Then they led him away to crucify him.

## The Crucifixion of Jesus

³²As they went out, they came upon a man from Cyrene named Simon; they compelled this man to carry his cross. ³³And when they came to a place called Golgotha (which means Place of a Skull), ³⁴they offered him wine to drink, mixed with gall; but when he tasted it, he would not drink it. ³⁵And when they had crucified him, they

divided his clothes among themselves by casting lots; ³⁶then they sat down there and kept watch over him. ³⁷Over his head they put the charge against him, which read, 'This is Jesus, the King of the Jews.'

³⁸Then two bandits were crucified with him, one on his right and one on his left. ³⁹Those who passed by derided him, shaking their heads ⁴⁰and saying, 'You who would destroy the temple and build it in three days, save yourself! If you are the Son of God, come down from the cross.' ⁴¹In the same way the chief priests also, along with the scribes and elders, were mocking him, saying, ⁴²'He saved others; he cannot save himself. He is the King of Israel; let him come down from the cross now, and we will believe in him. ⁴³He trusts in God; let God deliver him now, if he wants to; for he said, "I am God's Son."' ⁴⁴The bandits who were crucified with him also taunted him in the same way.

# The Death of Jesus

Sandro Botticelli · Lamentation of Christ · c. 1490

⁴⁵From noon on, darkness came over the whole land until three in the afternoon. ⁴⁶And about three o'clock Jesus cried with a loud voice, 'Eli, Eli, lema sabachthani?' that is, 'My God, my God, why have you forsaken me?' ⁴⁷When some of the bystanders heard it, they said, 'This man is calling for Elijah.' ⁴⁸At once one of them ran and got a sponge, filled it with sour wine, put it on a stick, and gave it to him to drink. ⁴⁹But the others said, 'Wait, let us see whether Elijah will come to save him.' ⁵⁰Then Jesus cried again with a loud voice and breathed his last. ⁵¹At that moment the curtain of the temple was torn in two, from top to bottom. The earth shook, and the rocks were split. ⁵²The tombs also were opened, and many bodies of the saints who had fallen asleep were raised. ⁵³After his resurrection they came out of the tombs and entered the holy city and appeared to many. ⁵⁴Now when the centurion and those with him, who were keeping watch over Jesus, saw the earthquake and what took place, they were terrified and said, 'Truly this man was God's Son!'

⁵⁵Many women were also there, looking on from a distance; they had followed Jesus from Galilee and had provided for him. ⁵⁶Among them were Mary Magdalene, and Mary the mother of James and Joseph, and the mother of the sons of Zebedee.

# The Burial of Jesus

⁵⁷When it was evening, there came a rich man from Arimathea, named Joseph, who was also a disciple of Jesus. ⁵⁸He went to Pilate and asked for the body of Jesus; then Pilate ordered it to be given to him. ⁵⁹So Joseph took the body and wrapped it in a clean linen cloth ⁶⁰and laid it in

his own new tomb, which he had hewn in the rock. He then rolled a great stone to the door of the tomb and went away. ⁶¹Mary Magdalene and the other Mary were there, sitting opposite the tomb.

## The Guard at the Tomb

⁶²The next day, that is, after the day of Preparation, the chief priests and the Pharisees gathered before Pilate ⁶³and said, 'Sir, we remember what that impostor said while he was still alive, "After three days I will rise again." ⁶⁴Therefore command the tomb to be made secure until the third day; otherwise his disciples may go and steal him away, and tell the people, "He has been raised from the dead," and the last deception would be worse than the first.' ⁶⁵Pilate said to them, 'You have a guard of soldiers; go, make it as secure as you can.' ⁶⁶So they went with the guard and made the tomb secure by sealing the stone.

## chapter TWENTY-EIGHT

# The Resurrection of Jesus

After the sabbath, as the first day of the week was dawning, Mary Magdalene and the other Mary went to see the tomb. ²And suddenly there was a great earthquake; for an angel of the Lord, descending from heaven, came and rolled back the stone and sat on it. ³His appearance was like lightning, and his clothing white as snow. ⁴For fear of him the guards shook and became like dead men. ⁵But the angel said to the women, 'Do not be afraid; I know that you are looking for Jesus who was crucified. ⁶He is not here; for he has been raised, as he said. Come, see the place where he lay. ⁷Then go quickly and tell his disciples, "He has been raised from the dead, and indeed he is going ahead of you to Galilee; there you will see him." This is my message for you.' ⁸So they left the tomb quickly with fear and great joy, and ran to tell his disciples. ⁹Suddenly Jesus met them and said, 'Greetings!' And they came to him, took hold of his feet, and worshipped him. ¹⁰Then Jesus said to them, 'Do not be afraid; go and tell my brothers to go to Galilee; there they will see me.'

# The Report of the Guard

¹¹While they were going, some of the guard went into the city and told the chief priests everything that had happened. ¹²After the priests had assembled with the elders, they devised a plan to give a large sum of money to the soldiers, ¹³telling them, 'You must say, "His disciples came by night and stole him away while we were asleep." ¹⁴If this comes to the governor's ears, we will satisfy him and keep you out of trouble.' ¹⁵So they took the money and did as they were directed. And this story is still told among the Jews to this day.

# The Commissioning of the Disciples

¹⁶Now the eleven disciples went to Galilee, to the mountain to which Jesus had directed them. ¹⁷When they saw him, they worshipped him; but some doubted. ¹⁸And Jesus came and said to them, 'All authority in heaven and on earth has been given to me. ¹⁹Go therefore and make disciples of all nations, baptising them in the name of the Father and of the Son and of the Holy Spirit, ²⁰and teaching them to obey everything that I have commanded you. And remember, I am with you always, to the end of the age.'

'Do not be afraid; I know that you are looking for Jesus who was crucified.

He is not here; for he has been raised ...'

'And remember, I am with you always, to the end of the age!'

# Lectio divina

*Lectio divina* (meaning 'divine reading' or 'holy reading') is an ancient method of paying attention to God's Word in Scripture in order to achieve a fuller understanding of the message and thus be better able to take it to heart in daily life. It was first practiced in the early Christian monasteries. Pope Benedict XVI said: 'I would like in particular to recall and recommend the ancient tradition of *lectio divina*: the diligent reading of Sacred Scripture accompanied by prayer brings about that intimate dialogue in which the person reading hears God who is speaking, and, in praying, responds with trusting openness of heart.'

*Lectio divina* is a particularly simple approach to prayer. It can be used individually or in groups. Ideally, you should choose the same time each day for this exercise and in a place free of distraction so that a daily habit will be learned.

So, choose a text of Scripture, something fairly brief and engaging. Then:

*Lectio* (read): Slowly read the text, being alert for God's Word to your life; notice what stands out for you or seems significant.

*Meditatio* (meditate): Read the text again. Pause and talk to God about what you are hearing. Meditation is like talking to God.

*Contemplatio* (contemplate): Read again. Now listen to and receive what God may be saying to you. Contemplation is like listening to God.

*Oratio* (pray): Recognise and pray whatever may be the deep desire of your heart.

Then some traditions add:

*Actio* (action): What does this study and prayer time call you to do? How will you take it to heart in your life now?

People from all walks of life are realising the benefits of this type of spiritual exercise. *Lectio divina* allows you to explore the deep wisdom of Scripture and to experience God in a very personal way.

# Index